I know of no church-planting pastor in America more pragmatically sensible, spiritually focused or scripturally motivated as Ralph Moore. To my awareness, he leads the team of those visionary and gifted leaders who "disciple and plant," "disciple and plant," "disciple and plant." I praise God for this book's availability. You'll find it all workable—no fluff, no puff, just good stuff for expanding the Kingdom.

DR. JACK W. HAYFORD
FOUNDING PASTOR, THE CHURCH ON THE WAY
CHANCELLOR, THE KING'S COLLEGE AND SEMINARY
VAN NUYS, CA

Having seen the Hope Chapel movement up close, I was thrilled to see Ralph Moore put on paper what he has been doing for years. All the Hope Chapels I have observed have Ralph's "love you as is" philosophy of ministry, backed by solid Bible teaching, spiritual worship and street-level social service. Behind the casual, laid-back ministry style is Ralph's (and hence the Hope Chapels') DNA— a genetic code that includes a ferocious commitment to multiplying the ministry through planting new churches. *Starting a New Church* gleans principles from that tenacity and helps those of us who want to start churches to "run with the vision" (Hab. 2:2). He also includes plenty of nuts and bolts to hold the vision together as we run. Ralph's critics call him a "church planting Nazi." He should wear that badge as a medal of honor from the King!

DANNY LEHMANN
HAWAII DIRECTOR, YOUTH WITH A MISSION
HONOLULU, HI

This practical and inspiring book has integrity because the author is living and doing what he writes. A significant part of my own ministry is sifting through all of the resources available, to find the best for church planters. This book will be a standard resource because Ralph provides the needed balance and integration of God-dependant faith with practical , strategic planning. While Ralph often speaks out of his own church planting experience, he is able to distill generic principles for all church planting models and situations. The reader will be blessed with countless gems such as: "Evangelism always means fishing the deep waters of human need." I highly recommend this book to denominational leaders with responsibility for church planting and to every church planter God has called into this thrilling and urgently needed ministry.

ALLEN E. LIKKEL
CHURCH PLANTING SPECIALIST,
CHRISTIAN REFORMED CHURCH OF NORTH AMERICA
SEATTLE, WA

Starting a New Church is a fresh and refreshing approach to church planting. In this work, Ralph Moore communicates vision that looks beyond what exists to what can exist—courage to reach beyond comfort to commission—and practical insights to both the strategic and the supernatural aspects of church planting.
I recommend this book not only to every person thinking about church planting, but to every established church and every pastor who needs a fresh vision for their own ministry. I wish that every church leader had Ralph's vision.

LINUS MORRIS
AUTHOR, THE HIGH IMPACT CHURCH
THOUSAND OAKS, CA

CONTENTS

PART 1
Thinking Through a Church Plant

PART 2
Designing the New Church

DEDICATION

This book is dedicated to the hundreds of

team members who have joined us in launching

new congregations since 1971. Their lives have resulted

in many people coming to know Jesus.

Published by Regal Books
From Gospel Light
Ventura, California, U.S.A.
Printed in the U.S.A.

Cover and interior design by Robert Williams
Edited by Steven Lawson

Library of Congress Cataloging-in-Publication Data

Moore, Ralph.
    Starting a new church / Ralph Moore.
        p. cm.
Includes bibliographical references.
    ISBN 0-8307-2966-6 (trade paper)
    1.   Church development, New.   I. Title.
    BV652.24 .M66 2002
    254' .1—dc21   2002008301

4 5 6 7 8 9 10 11 12 13 14 15 / 09 08 07 06 05 04

Rights for publishing this book in other languages are contracted by Gospel Light Worldwide, the international nonprofit ministry of Gospel Light. Gospel Light Worldwide also provides publishing and technical assistance to international publishers dedicated to producing Sunday School and Vacation Bible School curricula and books in the languages of the world. For additional information, visit www.gospellightworldwide.org; write to Gospel Light Worldwide, P.O. Box 3875, Ventura, CA 93006; or send an e-mail to info@gospellightworldwide.org.

STARTING A
New Church

RALPH MOORE

Regal

From Gospel Light
Ventura, California, U.S.A.

What Ralph brings to the church leaders of the twenty-first century are proven ideas wrapped in sound advice. He is a thinker and is rock solid in practicing what he preaches. In today's trendy church-growth culture pastors are willing to pay thousands of dollars to sit at dinner with successful church gurus to gather secrets for turning their meager ministries into mega ones. Ralph cuts through the fluff and fantasy with practical instruction, while asking hard-hitting questions. If you are ready and willing to embrace a church-plant mentality, then this book will launch you into exciting new territory.

BILL STONEBRAKER
PASTOR, CALVARY CHAPEL HONOLULU
HONOLULU, HI

Ralph is my hero! He is the church planting expert of the Western world. And his book is both a practical guide and a super faith-builder. If you read this book, then you will begin to believe you can plant a church.

STEVE SJOGREN
LAUNCHING PASTOR, VINEYARD COMMUNITY CHURCH
CINCINNATI, OH

This book is literally crammed with practical ideas from one of the most effective church planters in the world today. I am so grateful that Ralph has finally put his wisdom into print for the rest of us. This book is no theory, it works! God has used Ralph's ministry to bring thousands to Christ and to start hundreds of churches. I just wish he'd written it years before I struggled through my first years of planting Saddleback. Reading it could have spared me from a lot of mistakes.

RICK WARREN
PASTOR, SADDLEBACK CHURCH
AUTHOR, *THE PURPOSE DRIVEN CHURCH*
LAKE FOREST, CA

Ralph's great wisdom is communicated as he shares stories from his vast church planting experiences. Ralph identifies three impediments to rapid multiplication of the church: required seminary training, a dedicated building for church services and full-time remuneration for pastors. He offers practical insights and solutions for each one. A must-read for anyone considering church planting.

REV. STEVE OGNE
CRM CHURCH MULTIPLICATION
SOMIS, CA

Ralph Moore has become one of the most prolific and creative church planters of our generation. In reading this book you will find Ralph to be more of a practitioner than a theorist. Although he is passionate about multiplying churches, he readily acknowledges the challenges and pain that accompany the process of establishing new congregations. I advise my fellow pastors never to embark on the church planting adventure without talking to Ralph or reading everything he has written on the subject. He is, quite frankly, one of the best.

PAUL RISSER
PRESIDENT, INTERNATIONAL CHURCH OF THE FOURSQUARE GOSPEL
LOS ANGELES, CA

As a church planter who planted and remained in that church for nearly five decades now, I wish to commend Ralph Moore as one of this generation's most successful church planters. He has systematically placed before us the best "how-to" manual you can find. He helps us to realize more clearly that the greatest churches are yet to be built!

DR. ROBERT H. SCHULLER
PASTOR, THE CRYSTAL CATHEDRAL
GARDEN GROVE, CA

PART 3
Planting the New Church

PART 4
Anticipating the Future

PREFACE

Starting a new church is a great adventure. People join the process for various reasons. Prospective pastors usually initiate the process out of a sense of calling. Some people join a church-planting team because they are bored with status quo Christianity. Many will join the project out of loyalty to and friendship with the prospective pastor. Others attach themselves to a new church because they want to escape a congregation that no longer meets their needs. A few may help start a new church with hopes of learning enough to duplicate the process at a later date. Each one of these is a valid motive.

Whoever you are and whatever your drive, this book offers support for your journey. It is a mixture of scriptural insights and lessons learned from hard-won personal experience and Spirit-driven victories of lots of people. I am hopeful that you will find it practical and the advice easy to implement. In that sense it will benefit you greatly. It should provide a practical tool for a team to study together on the way to planting a new congregation or during those first few months after a church is birthed. I hope that this book will ensure the success of every church planter who reads it and works through the checkpoints at the end of each chapter.

The book is not, however, a final answer; nor does it claim to be the "right way" to plant a church. The nearest example we have of a right way is that of Jesus who planted the church He left behind in Jerusalem on the day of His ascension.

As an author, I tend to tell stories of success. As you read these stories, you would do well to remember that for every victory there is also a rough spot in the road. Let me also caution you not to be overwhelmed by my tendency to report about a large number of churches that my friends and I have planted. We have been at this for a long time. Perseverance is our great ally. We have known success mostly because we have kept at the task. We have no secret formula other than a belief that every church should be about the business of planting churches—repeatedly. Over time, when that belief is put into practice, it results in numerical success. In fact, our greatest successes come downstream from our planting efforts. The churches that we planted have planted others—in several cases many others.

My prayer is that you see the same success in your church plant. May you realize your purpose and then pass it on to others over several generations of churches. May God's grace accompany you on your adventure.

PART 1

THINKING THROUGH
a Church Plant

CHAPTER 1

CALLING:
WHY I PLANT CHURCHES

People often ask why I expend so much energy on planting churches. They usually question the sacrifices my family, the members of my church and I make in the process. Sometimes they bluntly query, "Wouldn't you be pastoring a larger church if you just stopped giving people away?" I always answer, "Yes, but I would touch fewer people."

THE DREAM IS BORN

The idea came to me when I was 19. I had been assigned the yard-care duties as part of a summer church-planting project in Gresham, Oregon. The inspiration struck while I was weeding the lawn in front of East Hill Church's tiny sanctuary.

As a way to kill boredom, I sang while I worked. That day the old Charles Wesley hymn "O for a Thousand Tongues to Sing" came to mind. It is a prayer for a thousand voices to sing God's praises. The best way to assemble such a choir, or so I thought, would be to evangelize a thousand people. But with very little experience in ministry, I nearly tossed this idea aside, reasoning that it would be impossible to complete such a task in my lifetime. Then I jumped to the concept of starting several churches. I view this mental leap through the prism of revelation, although it did not—and still does not—seem the least bit ethereal.

There were two reasons why I initially dismissed the idea that I could ever evangelize large numbers of people or pastor a large church. First, at the time my denomination (Foursquare) only had three congregations of more than 1,000 members. The second reason held deeper implications: I simply did not believe in myself.

The youngest in my class, I was always the last kid picked for playground sports. My family did not have a lot of money, while my friends' parents did. I had no musical talent and was frightened of speaking in public. There were many reasons to feel that I did not have what it would take to lead a large congregation, but if I multiplied churches these issues would be resolved.

As I daydreamed in that garden, I devised a plan. Over a lifetime I would gradually move down the Oregon coast and plant seven churches. I would progress from town to town like the apostle Paul did during his missionary journeys. Hopefully, after spending five to seven years in each small city, I would leave behind a trail of functioning congregations. The intent was to leverage my limited gifts by planting numerous churches.

GOD HAD BIGGER PLANS

Nearly four decades later, my purpose remains unchanged, but the goal has grown. The Oregon coast was too small for the vision

God communicated that day in the churchyard. Planting seven churches, one after the other, was a good idea but tiny compared to the plan God eventually revealed. Today I do pastor a large congregation, but I have found that I can best advance my gifts, time and mentoring abilities when I multiply the church.

This larger course started in the autumn of 1971 when I met with 12 people in Manhattan Beach, California—the first Hope Chapel. At this writing, that initial church plant has blossomed into the Hope Chapel movement and includes more than 200 congregations. The network extends to five continents, and it would take a sizeable stadium to hold the members of all its churches, most of whom will never meet one another in this life.

Rapid multiplication from a single location, as we have seen at Hope Chapel, seems close to what Jesus had in mind for the 12 apostles when He sent them from Jerusalem to Judea and Samaria and then to the ends of Earth (see Acts 1:8). The model has worked for me. It has allowed one man with limited skills and gifts to reach and get a message of hope to tens of thousands of people, most of whom he will never meet.

WE PLANT OUR FIRST CHURCH

When the first Hope Chapel was birthed in Manhattan Beach I was ready and excited, but also fearful. However, when God presented my coworkers and me with an opportunity to launch a second congregation—only a short time after we had started the first—I balked. Although the concept was biblical, it was too "far out," even for a hippie pastor in the 1970s. Tradition still ruled in my heart. Church planting, in my mind, had to operate out of a denominational seedbed, not spring forth from a local congregation. Operating under my preconceived wishful thinking I was supposed to disciple people and send them to seminary. The denomination would turn them into church planters.

We Break from Tradition

At that time my circle of fellowship had no concept of churches planting churches, nor could it accept pastors mentoring
other pastors. Fortunately the person I spoke to in the denominational hierarchy had a more flexible wineskin than I. He told
me that he hoped his daughter would one day marry and bear
him grandchildren, but he had no right to dictate where and
when she would have children. He observed that our church
was pregnant with our first daughter church and said that he
had no right to interfere with the process. If we planted a
church, he would find a way to widen the denomination's poli-
ty to embrace it.

He was a very wise man. When he stretched the denomination's wineskin, he stretched ours, too. Our vision grew, and
many new churches exist today because of his counsel. I now live
in the hope that the seven churches I envisioned as a 19-year-old
will expand to 500 by the time I retire. Church planting as much
as pastoring has become my calling—but not mine alone. You are
reading this book for a reason. I believe the reason is that God
wants to stretch your wineskin and accomplish through you far
more than you dare to imagine.

CHURCH PLANTER'S CHECKLIST

1. What is there in the author's testimony that resonates
   with the vision God has put in your heart?
2. Write three to five paragraphs that recount your personal vision as it relates to church planting.
3. What will it take for you to multiply many churches
   within your current church or denominational family?

CHAPTER 2

MISSION:
WHY SHOULD *YOU* PLANT A CHURCH?

Today Christian leaders peer through a maze of exciting megachurch testimonies and pesky statistics as we search for the keys to success. The Christian media overflows with victory story after victory story. Yet whenever surveyors such as George Barna tally the numbers, the results show the Church yielding ground, both numerically and spiritually. We seem to be losing the war for the hearts of the people of this world.

Most established churches serve their constituents well. But, on the whole, we are not winning over the unchurched. As we struggle to grow individual congregations, the percentage of Christians within the general population is shrinking. Our cities resemble urban donut holes. Suburbanites embrace Christianity while inner-city dwellers look to other options. Surprisingly, many members of rising generations of Americans live in ignorance of Jesus Christ and do not possess a sense of moral absolutes. We need a new approach, because the old way only maintains the status quo, thereby diminishing the overall size and influence of the Church. *Aggressive church planting has the potential to reverse this trend.*

WE CAN LEARN FROM LINCOLN

President Abraham Lincoln stood at a severe disadvantage through much of the U.S. Civil War. His generals refused to fight—they would not engage the enemy. At the beginning of the war, military leaders recommended a defensive plan. They believed guarding Union territory and containment of the South would eventually calm the conflict. Lincoln disagreed. Between 1861 and 1863, he replaced four successive generals-in-chief and, despite the roar of protests from important people, he finally settled on Ulysses S. Grant. Living up to his nickname, "Unconditional Surrender," Grant displayed courage and tactical skill through several commanding victories. His detractors complained, however, because he labored under a record of heavy battlefield casualties. It was also rumored that he had been drunk during some of his battles. When confronted about his choice of Grant, Lincoln dismissed criticism by saying, "I can't spare this man. He fights!"[1]

Today we are in a war of another sort. Like Lincoln, we need officers who will take the battle to the enemy. We are called not to defend turf, but to invade enemy territory. Our objectives must include entire cities. Our tactics should differ from much of our treasured tradition. Our mission is not to kill but to spare lives.

LET'S CONSIDER THE REASONS

Have you ever questioned your friends about their prayers for spiritual awakening? I have. I find that most Christians request more of whatever they already experience at church. They also expect this to come juiced with a sensory awareness of the Holy Spirit. They ask for their relatives and friends to come to the Lord. Some pray that the gospel would change their culture, but few petition for entire cities, even countries to embrace the Savior. If we are going to win the world, then we need more than a refilling with the Spirit. We need far more labor in the harvest (see Matt. 9:35-38). We need more churches as frontline bases in the spiritual conflict.

There are many reasons why you *should* be thinking about planting a church. In the paragraphs that follow, I examine a few of the better reasons.

Helpful Fact: One American denomination recently found that 80 percent of its converts came to faith in Jesus in churches less than two years old. Like General Grant, church planters produce results—they put aside traditional methods and find new ones to effectively organize their ministries and evangelize their cities. *New congregations pay off in effective evangelism and church growth!*

New Churches Provide Superior Results

As I have already noted, in my early years of ministry I sent many church-planting teams out from Manhattan Beach. Then, in 1983, I moved a team of 30 people from California to Hawaii to plant a church myself. That church subsequently planted others. When we moved to Hawaii, our goal was to evangelize 1 percent of the populace, bringing them into newly planted congregations in one decade. Just before we left California, my team members and I were told twice to stay home.

Both so-called encouragers cited the need for *existing* churches to grow as the reason we should not start a new one. Over the past two decades we have planted about 30 churches in Hawaii, all stemming from that original congregation. Thousands of people find the Lord each year in those congregations. Others, encouraged by our successes, have begun planting churches. Spillover growth occurs every time we establish churches in other states or countries. Ironically, the churches of those two critics do show growth, but the increase does not total 200 new members in nearly 20 years. If we had stayed in California, our Hope Chapel movement would not have expanded as it has, and even the churches of our critics might not have grown as much as they did. (Incidentally, the leaders of those two churches have since attended our seminars.)

More Churches Produce a Better Harvest

I wish everyone who has come to Christ through the efforts of the Hope Chapel movement would also stay and grow with us— but they do not. Despite our best efforts, we cannot adjust to meet the needs of everyone we encounter.

I once heard a children's song titled "Different Strokes for Different Folks." The wisdom of that tune extends to churches. It is easier to retain a convert if the new Christian has lots of options. This is true within a given church and when there are many other churches from which a person can choose.

Just because a person is evangelized by a certain group does not mean that the new believer is going to feel comfortable in close fellowship with it. We often lead people to Christ whose tastes in worship, teaching or programs vary from what we offer—different strokes for different folks. At Hope Chapel, we are *glad* when we can refer people to other churches that can more adequately meet their needs. When we look at evangelism in this light, it becomes clear that the more churches in a community, the more chances there are for people truly to find a place where they fit into the Body of Christ.

New Churches Speak Best to the Next Generation
Perhaps our greatest responsibility is to evangelize our own generation. After that comes the need to pass the baton of Christianity to our children and grandchildren. This task can prove to be daunting. Language, music, clothing and lifestyles change over time. They tend to make our wineskins less flexible and unable to hold the new wine that can attract a new generation.

Decisions emerge quickly in new congregations; the process moves more and more slowly as a church grows older. Members of church plants find fresh ways of expressing worship and truth without resorting to an endless array of committee meetings. They naturally tend to speak the language of the founding generation yet are able to avoid offending God-loving people from other generations. Although every congregation will be at least somewhat multigenerational, we need new churches that are focused on the needs of each new generation.

New Churches Move the Gospel Across Cultural Lines
Let's face it: my mother's cooking tastes better to me than that stuff your mom makes. We all have our own propensities and like to be with people who hold similar opinions. Much of our view of the world derives from our culture, including our food, music, dance, hand gestures and parenting styles—the list of preferences seems infinite. This principle is the same when it comes to picking a church. We tend to go where we are most comfortable.

Having lots of new churches simplifies evangelistic efforts among people of varying cultures and tastes. Getting people

together with others who think the way they think makes it easier to present the gospel in a way that makes sense to a spiritually
hungry individual. It is simpler because the gospel gets communicated in a culturally friendly manner and at a personal level.

New Churches Can Open Doors for Very Poor People

Moreover, we all feel comfortable with people of our own economic standing. This is why poor people do not flock to middle-
class Christian churches. Neither do the extremely wealthy go to
inner-city congregations.

This stratification compounds itself through a factor sociol-
ogists call "redemption and lift." Poorer people who find the
Lord improve their financial situation through disciplined living and the wisdom of the Holy Spirit. Eventually they see success on the job, earn more money and move into more costly
neighborhoods. These people often continue to worship with
their old congregation, but the natural lines of communication
break down and they quickly become outsiders. As these people
grow older, the gospel becomes confined to their hearts. As a
result, in the old neighborhood, members of the next generation
come to view Christianity as a religion for the elderly and seek
other spiritual options. *We need a new witness aimed at younger people in every neighborhood and town.*

New Churches Offer a Better Use of Resources

Land, buildings and programs are expensive—sometimes they are
wasteful uses of resources. Yet their purchase and construction
are somehow becoming the benchmarks of congregational
success. Discussions about mortgage interest rates, square-
footage and staff salaries abound at pastor's conventions like
stock market conquests at a cocktail party. Meanwhile, new congregations grow explosively in borrowed or rented facilities with
minimal overhead and a mostly volunteer staff. A wise invest-

ment counselor might treat us to a figurative look in the mirror over our use of resources reflected against the results we seek.

Freshly Planted Churches Present Leadership Development Opportunities

Adequate leadership is a monstrous need in every church. For this reason, church planters become excellent recruiters and innovators, or their churches die. The results of their recruitment and training efforts generally spill over into neighboring churches, missions and parachurch ministries.

Every church labors to develop and disciple new leaders, but new congregations do it faster. They are also forced to raise more leaders per capita into significant positions than long-established congregations that have already filled these positions or that look to seminary graduates to fill them. As a result, new churches add primary leaders to the Christian community at a much faster rate than older congregations do. This harvest of leaders alone more than justifies a cry for accelerated efforts to birth churches.

New Churches Rarely Haggle over Manifestations of the Holy Spirit

We all become set in our ways *and* in our interpretation of truth. During the Jesus movement of the 1970s, young people began to raise their hands during worship, speak in tongues at prayer services and clap their hands in church. Their elders were often aghast at such behavior. Many congregations were thrown into confusion only to have the problems resolved by what I will call grand-elders—people who were old enough to have experienced a move of the Holy Spirit in the past.

These gray-haired bearers of wisdom calmed the waters when they could. Meanwhile, younger congregations, unfettered by years of tradition and experience, plunged swiftly into the waves of spiritual awakening. Church planters and their congregations never even held discussions about these activities, because they did not have to line up with existing traditions—they had none. Newer churches can focus their energies on evangelism because they have fewer theological issues to resolve.

Established Congregations Can Grow Fastest by Simple Multiplication

A sheepfold tends to operate at or near the shepherd's maximum leadership capacity. When a natural, economic or spiritual disaster robs a church of large numbers of people, a healthy congregation will usually see enough unbelievers come to faith in its services to regain equilibrium. When too many new converts come aboard too quickly, the average church leadership structure either collapses or opens like a sieve letting people out until equilibrium reasserts itself. A leadership team's vision and ability, centering in the pastor, dictate the size of the church. It is hard to teach new tricks to old dogs. Millions of dollars and man-hours invested in church-growth seminars annually attest to this fact. We listen to the best, but we have a hard time digesting what we have heard. Church planting solves this problem by letting the pastor and congregation simply duplicate themselves rather than be forced to relearn church-growth principles and to redefine how they do ministry.

Church Planting Was the Chosen Tool of Jesus and the Apostles

The New Testament points toward the rapid deployment of congregations as the model Jesus intended for building His Church. It took eight years for the gospel to escape Jerusalem. But when it did, it sparked a church-planting movement in Antioch that quickly spread throughout the Roman Empire.

Jesus delineated the task just before He ascended into heaven. The disciples were now called apostles. This move modified the purpose of their assignment. The parlance shifted from a term meaning "learner" to one suggesting that the person who bears it is an "ambassador." The name change alone should have helped them understand that they were to *go* and *make* disciples. Jesus was not subtle about this. He gave the apostles specific instructions and sent them from Judea into Samaria and finally to the ends of Earth. Yet from all appearances the team never really made any progress toward the rest of the world until their work took on the trappings of a church-planting movement. When leaders finally did reach out to the world, they planted churches. Their primary strategy was rapid multiplication of congregations.

Aggressive Church Planting Works

After three frustrating years, President Lincoln discovered Grant. Before that time he cajoled generals, wrote letters begging for action and even designed one battle plan himself. The rise of Grant allowed Lincoln to return to the business of running the country. If this small bit of American history carries one strong lesson for us, it is that of creative abandonment: Forsake what does not work for what does. With that in mind, you need to discover whether you have what it takes to multiply the Church.

CHURCH PLANTER'S CHECKLIST

1. Can you identify unmet needs in your target community that might be met by a newly planted church?
2. How would your new church impact your mother church? State negative as well as positive responses.

3. In your target community, what opportunities exist that only a new church could exploit?

Note

1. Donald T. Phillips, *Lincoln on Leadership* (New York: Warner Books, 1992), p. 124.

CHAPTER 3

ASSIGNMENT:

ARE *YOU* READY TO PLANT A CHURCH?

Kaz Sekine planted a successful church in the heart of Tokyo. However, from the start, it was not easy. Unable to find space to rent, he set up folding chairs and held services outdoors in Shinjuku Park, which is near thousands of coffee shops and nightspots that attract a myriad of young adults. On the first Sunday, a typhoon hit, but they went ahead with services. Thus the church was born under umbrellas. Eighteen months later, the congregation moved into a nightclub. On the last Sunday in the park, like the first, umbrellas were needed. This time they popped up to protect worshipers from a snowstorm. Innovative thinking allowed my friend and his congregation to prevail where others would have failed.

Not everyone can plant a church. New ventures contain the risk of failure and demand a high level of operational faith. A journey in uncharted waters requires resourceful and flexible people who have lots of team support. Sometimes it even requires umbrellas.

How Do You Measure Up?

Planting a church is not that difficult. If you are reading this book, you *probably* have the right tools and temperament. Most likely you have assembled plans and a team that will ensure success. God is certainly on your side as His plan centers on the birth of new congregations. My goal in this chapter is to ask you to review the areas where you will be vulnerable to Satan's attack. A careful assessment of your own position is a great defense against unguarded failure.

Let's Examine Your Wineskin

Jesus likened the work of the Spirit to new wine that is stored best in flexible new wineskins (see Matt. 9:17). In this analogy, He was talking about religious systems.

We can think of a church as a new or an old wineskin, depending upon how long it has existed and whether it has become encumbered by tradition. But this might be a misleading approach. Have you ever stopped to realize that a church is usually a reflection of its senior leadership? If this observation is true, then it would be possible to plant a new church that functions as an old wineskin. The issue is not *age* as much as *flexibility*. Do you embody new-wineskin flexibility? If you are contemplating a church plant, your leadership style should be malleable enough to meet challenges ranging from scarce resources and an ever-changing culture to typhoons and snowstorms.

Let's take a little test.

Are You Flexible?

How do you respond to unexpected changes? If you are flexible, then sudden challenges will not blow away your plans. Instead, you will see the hurdles as opportunities to be creative and to establish the unique personality of your church.

In Hawaii, we negotiated an agreement to lease an entire floor of a new office building. Two weeks before we were to arrive, the company that managed the facility reneged on its verbal agreement. My partners and I immediately flew to Oahu to make new arrangements. We searched everywhere, but public schools, parks and even a Chinese restaurant that had a banquet room turned us down. Determined not to accept defeat, we eventually planted our new church under a tree at the beach. The litany of rejections simply made the task more exciting. We chose to be flexible and enjoyed watching God provide an innovative solution.

What would you do if you had to find new facilities on very short notice?

Are You an Original Thinker?

Can you embrace innovative ideas and new paradigms? Do you look at processes from a variety of different angles? If you can, you will be able to differentiate your new church from every other congregation in town. A fresh approach gives people something positive to talk about.

Each time we plant a Hope Chapel, I try to stimulate the leadership team to rethink every potential activity in light of two questions:

- What are we trying to accomplish?
- What is the *best* way to do it?

When I ask these questions, I always hope the church planters come up with better ways of launching their ministry than the ones they learned from me. And whenever they do, I copy them.

For example, I learned from the former youth pastor at my church. Mike Kai took the task of leading a dying congregation we had planted on the other side of the island. He placed radio spots on mainstream stations to announce the changes. In six months, the church grew 700 percent! You can be sure that future Hope Chapel church plants will include radio advertisements.

What can you do better or more ingeniously than your mother church?

Do You Have What It Takes?

What fruit have you borne that makes you think you will be successful as a church planter?

Planting a new congregation is all about leadership. You will need to gather a group of strangers and mold them into a team capable of recruiting others to follow the Great Commission. It is not advisable to try this in a new and perhaps hostile environment until you have proven your ability to succeed in the relative comfort of a well-established congregation.

As I write, Kaala Souza and his wife are preparing to plant a church in Honolulu. They want to attract young adults and have secured a nightclub for their services. Kaala is another of our former youth pastors and has overseen our worship department. Working bivocationally, Kaala has recruited and organized a smooth-running team, operating it as a network of small-group Bible studies, and all along he has maintained a successful career as a marketing strategist. Both his past and current track records recommend him as a church planter.

What have you done that is predictive of a successful church plant?

Are You Driven by a Vision?

Do you possess an unavoidable urge to start a new congregation?

If you can live without this project, you probably should. The best church planters easily qualify for Peter Drucker's descriptive, "monomaniac with a mission."[1] They are driven by a call similar to the ones given to the apostle Paul and the Old Testament prophets. These are the people who can run their blood pressure up 10 points just by poring over a map of potential meeting sites.

One time I spent an hour with an ex-convict who became a Christian while in jail. He knew of me from a daily radio broadcast. For him, prison became a place of nurture and discipleship under the tutelage of an excellent chaplain. Upon "graduation" he joined one of Hope's daughter churches and eventually felt a call to plant a new church in a drug-infested neighborhood on a nearby island. His eyes filled with tears as he showed me a map on which he had marked all of the crack houses and shooting galleries. The man literally lives to take the gospel to people whose lives are being stolen by Satan, the destroyer. This former inmate is a monomaniac on a mission.

What do you live for?

Is Anyone Listening?

How well do you lead in your present circumstances? Do your ideas and observations carry weight with your peers and elders? Can you sell your ideas well enough to rally a team and take them into uncharted territory?

A leader is defined by his or her followers. Are they enthusiastic? Or are they satisfied with the status quo? Or are they a gang of malcontents? The American Revolution was led by the latter.

A hard look at your disciples will tell you volumes about whether you should start a church. I know one man who is a very good Bible study teacher. He leads people to the Lord and disciples them. But his followers never lead others to the Lord. Therefore, they would not make a good church-planting team. My advice to him would be to remain involved in the large church and continue to provide useful small-group ministry leadership.

What are the characteristics of the people who follow you?

Are You Connected?

Do you have a church-planting team in place or the ability to build one? Is there a parent group or church where the corporate culture will lend itself to help you?

The New Testament presents church planting as a team affair. The team members may not all move to the new location. Some will support the new church from afar. Wherever they live, your team should stand with you in prayer, fellowship and financial support.

My wife and I planted our first church with the help of a dozen people. We had little financial support other than our personal savings. We survived by God's generous grace.

Do your close friends support your vision? Are you connected to a peer group of leaders who will stick with you? Will these people lend you ideas and support you when you feel overwhelmed? Are they willing to move into the adventure and stand by your side?

Can You Lead into Unknown Territory?

Are you comfortable with a break from tradition? Can you carry others into the uncharted waters of an inventive new church culture?

The most successful church plants differentiate themselves from *both* the existing churches in the community *and* from the ideas most non-Christians hold about church.

Joshua and Caleb knew how difficult it is to break from tradition. When they returned from their spying trip, they were unable to move the Jewish people forward with enough faith to counteract the risk of invasion—40 years later they were up to the task. During those intervening years, they developed new leadership skills through hands-on experience. As 80-year-old men, they had grown in the competence that they had lacked on the first trip into the Promised Land.

Are you seasoned enough to undertake the task of planting a new and different church? Simply put, are you ready?

Can You Hold Your Own Under Fire?

Has your personal experience prepared you to confront problems and bring undisciplined people into fruitful service to our Lord?

A new church can be a magnet that attracts disgruntled Christians who have a history of conflict in other churches. My observations over the years tell me that more new churches fold from an inability to confront disruptive people than from any other cause.

My own life was miserable until I learned to confront in love. I would avoid talking with difficult people. This failure on my part inadvertently gave them free rein over the church. I learned to overcome this with the help of Don Stewart, whom I had hired to join our church staff. I was impressed by his loyalty, but intimidated by his management skills and employment experience. He had worked on the executive design team for the McDonnell Douglas DC-10.

At our church, I was his boss on paper, but he was mine when it came to me waffling over confrontation. He held my feet to the fire whenever I complained about a difficult person. Inevitably, he would look me directly in the eyes and ask, "What have you done to solve this problem? What did you say to this person?" I gradually began to take on difficult issues I had once avoided and, to my surprise, I found that many of these "problem people" simply lacked direction and boundaries to channel their passions. Don taught me to confront strong people and to set our church free to embrace them as potential leaders.

Are you comfortable enough in confrontation to be in a position in which it will likely happen?

Do You Take the Longer View?

Do you stick with the projects you start? Do you turn over leadership to others too soon? What do you do when a project fails?

The Bible often notes perseverance. Joseph remained *steady* in prison. David *never abandoned* Samuel's prophecies about him while on the run from Saul. Jesus *continued* with the few while the many abandoned him. The apostles *continued* to preach, even while they were being persecuted. Paul *remained faithful* even though the crowd in Jerusalem did not appreciate his message. Good planning and hard work *still* lead to prosperity, but hasty shortcuts lead to poverty (see Prov. 21:5).

I once knew a man who loved starting ministries in a growing church. He had great ideas. The efforts he launched always touched a nerve of human need. The only problem was that he would turn over the new ministry to one of his disciples several months before that person was actually ready for the task. Most of these ventures failed. My friend abandoned them in the name of empowerment. But really he had eyes only for the short-term.

A few years ago he called to tell me that he was leaving his job to plant a new church. I asked him if he planned to make a lifelong commitment to the new congregation. If he did not, I suggested that he help someone else plant a church and keep his job. He assured me that he would be in the new church until he retired. Instead, within two years he became bored with what was a quite successful church plant. As he had done in other ventures, he handed the church off to an ill-prepared follower, leaving that person to oversee a demoralized congregation. The people felt abandoned by the leader they had chosen to follow. Last I heard the well-intentioned church-planting pastor was trying to get his old job back in the secular marketplace.

Helpful Hint: If there is one predictor of success, or at least a common characteristic in church planters, it has been that the good ones are voracious readers. Well-read people tend to be able to find a solution to any problem and they always seem to have a fresh supply of ideas. Some of my best church-growth ideas have come from secular history and science texts.

Contrast that story with the young man who started a congregation in a New England town only to watch it fail. He merely moved 15 miles down the road and started another church, capitalizing the project with the last of his personal funds. Seven years and three daughter churches later, he is a marvelous success. The only difference between these two men is the ability of the second man to stay focused on a single goal for a longer period of time.

To which man do you relate?

CHURCH PLANTER'S CHECKLIST

1. On a scale of 1 to 10, rate yourself as an original thinker.
2. On a similar scale, rate yourself in terms of flexibility.
3. List three confrontations in which you faced an adversary and prevailed with a win-win solution.
4. Who follows you? List the 12 people who are most influenced by your life. Prioritize the list.

5. What is the shortest time you have held on to a new
project? Would you have enjoyed greater success if
you stuck around for a longer time? Why did you
leave the project when you did?

Note

1. Thomas J. Peters and Robert H. Waterman, Jr., *In Search of Excellence* (New
York: Warner Books, 1982), p. 225.

CHAPTER 4

GUIDANCE:
DO YOU KNOW WHERE YOU ARE GOING AND WHY?

I have personally planted two congregations, and I believe that each was born in the heart of God. He communicated His ideas to me through unusual spiritual experiences. The first church jumped into being while I was praying for another position. God simply asked me what I would do if the opportunity came to plant a church in a community that I really liked. The second church plant pulled me away from that first congregation. That time I actually *saw* a vision—pretty rough stuff for a guy who is skeptical of most visions.

But I firmly believe every new church must be a product of the Holy Spirit's design and the surrendered life of an individual. For this to happen there needs to be revelation. While guidance can come through a supernatural word or vision from God, it should *also* be a product of prayerful research and planning. The ideal church plant is like a river swollen with the flow of these two streams.

HAS GOD SPOKEN TO YOU?

Since you are reading this book, you probably lose sleep over the idea of planting a church. But have you heard from God on this matter? If so, are you willing to come out and admit it? Or are you feeling shy, afraid that people will think you are a little off balance for cataloging yourself in the same category as Ezekiel, Isaiah and Amos? Remember, those guys had revelations and looked pretty strange to the unbelievers in their day. Do not sweat over public opinion. You do not need to share every thought with your friends. But you should be willing to identify revelation as such, at least to yourself.

How Can You Identify God's Revelation?

What should you expect to hear from God? He speaks in many ways, but often in different ways to different people. You should expect Him to use biblical communication devices. The idea of a powerful word of wisdom or knowledge, an enlightening vision or a revelatory dream is not outside the realm of expectation. Beyond that, God will bring to mind ideas or experiences from your past.

As the Holy Spirit intersects your memories with exciting supernatural expressions and experiences you should embrace it as revelation. Some of my best church-planting tools came from youth-group experiences, both the ones I lived through as a teenager and those goofy ideas I forced on a youth group that I once led. These experiences commingled with the vision in my heart to seed our new church with fresh ways of approaching old problems. I believe God was at work orchestrating this entire process.

How Should You Respond to a Supernatural Word?

Have you already heard from God? Then you need to pay attention to what He is saying. Write down whatever you are sure He has revealed. Is much still unclear? Ask Him for clarification. James 1:5 reminds us, "If you need wisdom—if you want to know what God wants you to do—ask him, and he will gladly tell you. He will not resent your asking."

The supernatural vision that led to the transplantation of my family to Hawaii would have remained useless without the *vision statement* I wrote after I heard from God. Joining the spiritual experience to an ongoing research project was like injecting my body with caffeine after a night of insomnia.

I began by journaling the revelation and the random thoughts and ideas that followed. To the journal I added all of the demographic and geographic data I could find. Then I mixed in all of the church-planting ideas that stood out from my reading. I topped this off with a graduate thesis I found that focused on the 200-year history of church planting and evangelism in Hawaii.

I let the ideas simmer in my mind for a while, occasionally seasoning them with fresh data gleaned from other church planters. Months later, out popped a workable plan for a new congregation. That written plan became the guidebook for all we did during the first 10 months of our existence in Hawaii.

When God grants further insight, record it in your journal. What you write should anchor your thoughts to the sea bottom of revelation. It will help calm the waves of self-doubt and keep your mind from drifting about like an unsettled wave on the surface of the sea. In other words, you will sleep better if you have off-loaded spiritual experiences into a hidden diary.

Helpful Hint: For me, journaling was an indispensable part of the process. A formal business plan eventually grew out of my notes, but the informality of the journal freed my thoughts from the prison of rigidity. I found scribbling and immediately adding or crossing off fresh ideas in a notebook more productive than using a computer. But you should find a method that works best for you. The important act is to write it down.

WHAT DOES SCRIPTURE SAY?

What role does Scripture play in establishing the foundation of your church plant? In my circle of friends, we design new congregations around two Bible texts: Ephesians 4:10-13 and Acts 2:41-47. The one defines purpose for ministry, and hence the Church. The other lays out the architecture of New Testament church life.

I stumbled into the Ephesians passage because, in my earliest days of ministry, I simply did not understand that chapter of the New Testament. Somehow I did not get it when the professors went over it in Bible school. When I taught through Ephesians, it left me stumped for answers.

As I further researched the passage I discovered that in the mind of the apostle Paul leadership is designed to *equip* followers to *do* God's work. It was a short jump to the realization that the purpose for leadership is the same as the purpose for the overall organization. Rather than care for the saints, we are called to train them to serve others.

The message in Acts came while I was embarking upon a summer-camp assignment to teach teens the true nature of the Church. I was bored with the idea and tried to duck the task. As I reluctantly studied the lesson I discovered a biblical prototype for church life. The Acts model is viable in any setting or culture. When I intersected the recorded meeting places with the functions of the Early Church, I gained insight into reasons for success and failure that I had seen in contemporary churches. Further study caused a plan to leap off the pages of my Bible and into my journal.

As you read your Bible, the Lord will give you fresh insights into old passages. This is not redefining Scripture; rather, it is seeing how God's Word applies to your vision and your church plant. I remember reading Philippians for the umpteenth time and thinking how positive and uplifting Paul's message would be for any church. I wrote a note to that effect in my journal. Later I decided to start the new church with four weeks of Paul's words to the Christians in ancient Philippi. The positive nature of the message would imbue us with hope. The short length of the chapter gave me just enough time to assemble a bunch of strangers into something resembling a congregation before I launched a study of Acts. As I went through Acts, I intended to teach the newly assembled fellowship how a real church should work. I have now assembled those Scriptures into a teaching routine. They currently comprise the start-up curriculum for most of the churches Hope Chapel plants.

HERE ARE SOME HELPFUL INSIGHTS

Once you have a revelation and have written down your plan, it is time to start the actual church-planting process. As I have moved along the front lines of church planting, both as a planter and a sender, I have learned many valuable insights. In the remainder of this chapter I will share with you some practical tips to consider as you begin to unfold the vision God has given you for a new church.

Carefully Choose Some Friends You Can Trust

At some point early in the process you will want to share your plans with a few close friends. These should be the kinds of people who do not fear shooting straight with you, but will also love you enough to support a move that will cost them separation from you on a day-to-day basis.

During the early days of your planning process you must protect your calling. Do not discuss your thoughts with people who would be unable to grasp the idea of making strong sacrifices for the gospel. Those kinds of people will try to discourage you for their own selfish reasons. When discussing the church plant with positive-thinking friends, write down their insights and reactions. They will strengthen your treasure house of new ideas. These friends may help you develop a contact network of other people who feel that God has challenged them to reach the same city.

When I moved to Hawaii, some of the most important contributors to the effort came through (unbeknownst to me) contacts they had with some of my closest friends on the mainland. One guy, Sonny Shimaoka, planted a strong church on the Big Island. He had lived in Southern California and even visited our church. I hate to admit it, but at the time he was turned off by my style. Later a mutual friend insisted that I meet Sonny for breakfast while I was on one of my scouting trips to Oahu. It was to be my fourth breakfast meeting that day and I tried to beg off. When we finally did meet, we hit it off beautifully. I gained a worship leader, a cell-group leader, a strong family man, an eventual church planter and a lifelong friend—all because early in the process I took a trusted friend into confidence about my move.

Make Sure Your Spouse Is in Accord with Your Vision

God gifted me with a courageous wife. Her name is Ruby, and she *is* a jewel. We met in college and married while we were very young. Three times in our marriage we have uprooted from everything that gave us security for a move into relatively unknown situations. Each time, she has asked only that I am sure that the move is from God. To better understand her response, you need to know that every vacation and speaking trip is like a venture into a candy store for me. I see church-planting opportunities everywhere and would like to move to just about anywhere. My wife is *not* ready to move to all those places—only where the Lord is genuinely leading us.

Ruby's job is to ask the really hard questions and then to go to prayer on her own. She often comes up with fairly arcane Scriptures that have an uncanny bearing on the decision at hand. Her ability to oppose my goofy ideas while underscoring the solid ones makes her indispensable to the process of forward movement in every decision we face.

Without her wisdom, I never would have actually stepped into the world of church planting, especially the first time. She instinctively knew it was the right thing for us to do—even when the opportunity arose suddenly, without any previous clues to its existence. Just six months prior to starting the church in California the birth of our son caused us to lose 60 percent of our income (i.e., her salary). Our personal savings were solid, but they were all we had to complement an empty building that had come our way. I had prayed, asking the Lord to turn the entire decision upon her reaction to the *offer*. She simply said that she knew it was time and that we should go for it.

A marriage is two people leaving their parents, *cleaving* together and becoming *one flesh*. If you are married, both of you had better be ready to embrace church planting, or you should never move into the risks and challenges to your faith that you will face.

Choose Your Location

Once you confirm that God has called you to plant a church, you need to choose a location. Notice that I used the word "choose." I really think it is a choice in most cases. Even though I was pretty much directed by the Lord to come to Kaneohe, there was latitude in location choices once the team moved here. I want to emphasize *choice* because I believe we usually move about according to our choices, and it is only when we stall out (or make dumb decisions) that we should expect an overriding word from the Lord. Remember, Paul tried to plant churches in several cities before he saw the vision of the man from Macedonia (see Acts 16:6-10). When you make your choice, use common sense.

Match Your Calling to Real Needs

Your mind is important to the church-planting process; your feelings are less important. I get at least one letter a month from someone who, while on vacation, *felt* a calling to move to Hawaii and plant a church. Inevitably, the call is to one of the more beautiful and upscale neighborhoods or to a garden setting of indescribable loveliness. Never has one of these letters revealed a call to one of our poorer or drug-infested communities where life's pains would readily open hearts to the gospel. I usually assume that the inspiration of these letters comes more from bountiful flowers and beautiful sunsets than from the heart of God and the desire to establish new churches.

Jesus wept over lost people because they represented sheep without shepherds. His tears gave way to a request for laborers to engage fields that were overripe for harvest (see Matt. 9:37-38). Jesus' words mix sentiments of a calling with the demands of pressing needs. You should look for needs when trying to decide where to plant a church.

Unchurched communities abound in America. All of New England is hurting for leadership and many congregations lack pastors. But the fields of evangelism are ripening in this area of the country once white-hot with revival but long written off as spiritually dead. Several of my friends have had success in planting churches there. They think New England is *the* place to be if you want to experience a ground-shaking spiritual awakening. New York City is another place just waiting for aggressive church planters, as are most inner-city neighborhoods. Rural areas represent another field of opportunity. Working in these areas requires creative, innovative, go-against-the-grain leaders. This is because most of today's widespread methodology is best fit for suburban communities. Reaching both rural and inner-city communities requires inventive methods. Yet the need is there screaming at us like the man from Macedonia, "Come on over—we need what you have to offer."

Ask Yourself, *Will My Plan Really Work?*

Once you decide where to go, you need a plan, or at least a model, to guide you. For me the basic model is the cell church described in Acts 2:42-47. In this example, the large group meeting in the Temple set the tone for fellowship in the smaller home meetings. The apostles' teaching provided content for discussion and set boundaries for life application of the Word of God. Public meetings, or celebrations, gave great exposure to the gospel and allowed well-trained people to speak directly to the uninitiated. *Cells* meeting in homes added opportunity for personal intimacy and development of leaders who learned to be faithful over a few things.

Intimacy and personal growth are extremely important to members of postmodern generations. The church planted by Jesus in Jerusalem at the birth of Christianity answers these concerns with authenticity and simplicity. Twenty centuries later the New Testament model still works, and its many variations seem to get better results than anything else humankind has invented. But some circumstances present unique problems and opportunities.

If a small cell group is designed to balance out the larger assembly, what should you do if you start with a small crowd in a small town? What if you target a small populace of immigrants in a large city? Where should you house the celebration service if you are starting a church in urban Tokyo, where rents are imposingly high? How could you shape a church designed to reach families that depend upon two-and-one-half jobs per couple? Obviously holding more than one job severely limits discretionary time. How could the Internet help you to communicate with church members while holding fewer committee meetings? Questions such as these are trailheads to the innovation that can open doors for successful new churches. The answers to these questions will give you a good indication as to whether your church-plant idea will actually work.

LEARN A LESSON FROM PAUL

The answers to the questions raised in this chapter might come if we ask another: What would the apostle Paul do if he faced similar circumstances? We cannot really know what he would do, but using a successful church planter like Paul as a barometer will stretch our imaginations while keeping us within scriptural boundaries.

Paul did three things in every town where we can find a record of his church-planting activities. He preached, made disciples and appointed leaders from among the new converts, forming churches as he did. You and I have extreme latitude available to us when approaching these tasks. They are omnicultural, omnihistorical and can be done in any weather. It is our job to conceive how to do them best in the community where we choose to live and carry on the gospel of the Kingdom.

CHURCH PLANTER'S CHECKLIST

1. Is your idea to plant a church born of God, or does it come from peers, books, schooling or a glorious sunset?
2. Write out any supernatural encounter that led you to believe that God wants you to plant a church.
3. Can you list five key Scriptures that undergird your current vision?
4. What insights have you gleaned from your three closest friends? List the insights and your friends' names.
5. Does your spouse support this move?
6. Does your vision and call reflect genuine need in the city or neighborhood that you have chosen?

CHAPTER 5

SUPPORT:
WHERE SHOULD YOU
GO FOR HELP?

Money plays a big part in the process of launching a new church. There are several ways to approach the problem. Usually, though, funds invested in a new work are the product of preexisting relationships. Some supporters will join you on the front lines; others will stay behind or lend help from a great distance. Each type of support plays a vital role as you launch your ministry.

The *ideal* source of funding for a new church is a parent congregation whose members embrace the idea of extending evangelism through church planting. Other funding sources include denominations, wealthy or very committed patrons and the personal resources of the founding pastor. Each of these is valid under differing circumstances, and a combination of most or all of them are probably in your future. Let's look at the strengths and weaknesses of each source.

HOW CAN YOUR PARENT CHURCH HELP?

Organisms tend to reproduce in kind. Frogs beget frogs, churches beget churches, and denominational offices beget denominational offices. For this reason, the healthiest agency for church planting *is* a parent church. A group of Christians that births you will give sacrificially of their finances. Along with money, they will give their hearts. A parenting church will offer its name, wisdom, time and ongoing resource support as well. I like those advertisements that say, "American Express—don't leave home without it." In my mind, the same holds true for parent-church support. Do not leave home without it!

I once met with some people who were planning to move from the West Coast to Cambridge, Massachusetts. The goal was to start a new church that would target students at Harvard University. The church planter brought along his boss, the pastor of the church where he worked. The senior man asked me what the parent church should provide the young pastor on his way out the door. My answer surprised him. I turned to the younger man and advised him that the one asset he needed most was his senior pastor. Turning my attention back to the older man, I asked him if he was willing to walk the new turf with his protégé. He seemed a little startled to think the venture would require his physical presence. I explained that without his insights and wisdom, the actual invasion of new territory would be a lot harder for the man he had mentored. Much wisdom (and more financial help) would grow from the continued relationship of these two men and the ideas they cooked up together. This would not take lots of time. It would just require a spying trip prior to the launch date and a couple of trips to provide encouragement and insight during that crucial first year of congregational life.

Those men took my advice. They planted that church as a partnership. After scouting the location, they moved the new church away from Cambridge to an area more central to several colleges and built a thriving congregation. Having the senior leader on-site made a crucial difference in their planning. A parent church may not provide the deepest pockets, but it can offer the highest *quality* of support because of the already-existing relationships it brings to the project.

A Parent Participates in the Birthing Process

The staff and board of a parenting church provide much wisdom to the church planter in the planning and budgeting process. With the help of these people, instead of being a shot in the dark, a church-planting plan will root itself in reality.

At Hope Chapel, we take board involvement a step further. When we plant churches, our parent board always functions as the board of the new congregation for the first 12 months. This allows the new church to identify healthy leadership before installing its own board. In the first church I planted we jumped the gun when it came to board placement. We very quickly assembled a group from the most visible leaders in our emerging congregation. We suffered for two years because one person was motivated to bend the entire church to fit his own purposes.

A Parent Provides Nurture and Guidance

Parenthood does not end at the birth of a baby; it only blossoms. Parent-church pastors come into full bloom as mentors when the new church gets up and running. They become sounding boards for a host of important decisions. Regular meetings or phone conversations with a mentor are vital keys to building confidence in the heart of the church planter.

My own curious experience illustrates this. When I left California for Hawaii, I stayed in regular weekly contact with Zac Nazarian, the man who followed me in that pulpit in California. I had been his pastor for several years and was instrumental in discipling him into ministry. In a reversal of roles he became the sending pastor. Although I was in the Lord and in ministry many more years than he, his voice and advice became immensely valuable to me. I found comfort in our relationship because I was so vulnerable as the pastor of a yet-to-be-established church.

A Parent Knows When to Let Go

I love to read Acts. I once read the book on a daily basis for two years in an attempt to soak up Paul's missionary methods. What impressed me most—both then and now—was his ability to release leadership among people he barely knew. His worst-case example best shows his faith. He and Barnabas spent just two Sabbaths presenting the gospel in Antioch before being driven out of town and shaking the dust off their feet (see Acts 13:13-51). Yet this town was one of the places he revisited on his mission of strengthening believers, appointing elders and "turning them over to the care of the Lord, in whom they had come to trust" (Acts 14:23). Paul's ability to turn elders over to the care of the Lord is indicative of his faith in God. Paul viewed these young Christians as elders in the faith, although they were in Christ for only a few months.

At some point a parent church or organization must accept its offspring as its peer. The process becomes complete at this point. At Hope Chapel, we maintain a tight relationship with a church planter, both financially and relationally, during the first six months of the project. After that, we release any controls and view them as adult children capable of their own decisions in the care of the Lord.

> **Helpful Hint:** Be sure that you are in agreement with the leadership team at your parent church. They, not you, need to specify what is appropriate in terms of the resources you can take with you. This includes members, leaders and money. Do not assume anything. Talk over even the most minor detail. You cannot afford to alienate your parents. It also would be terrible to poison the well so that the mother church would not want to birth another congregation.

HOW CAN A DENOMINATION HELP?

Individual congregations have many issues on their agendas besides planting new congregations. Because they have so much to accomplish, they represent a finite source of financial supply. Usually a parent church must give money in partnership with other sources to ensure that ample funds are available for the task. The primary outside source of money is a denomination.

My denomination (Foursquare) works very hard to support church planters. It provides a great financial package along with a basic educational program to each new church. This is always a welcome enhancement to the work that we do from a local parenting church. Without the denominational funds we would find it impossible to plant as many churches as we do.

Honor Your Denominational Strings

Working within a denominational framework can be tricky for a new pastor. Local problems and opportunities dictate one set of behaviors, while denominational traditions demand another. As a church planter, you must learn to balance both realities.

You will soon find that your denomination's financial support comes with strings attached. If you receive this support, you will be required to participate in denominational functions. This can be frustrating. Officials will busy themselves with programs that focus on the forest while you try to nurture a single small tree. Sometimes you will see minimal relationship between the two. Differing expectations do not make one side right and the other wrong. They just call for clearer communication. You should spend time with your leaders *before* you plant a church. You need to ask them pointed questions about the expectations and boundaries that accompany their money. Understanding a denomination's place will keep church planters out of trouble.

Self-preservation is not the only motive at work. A full awareness of denominational objectives has helped many church planters discover just how useful denominational functions can be. There is a tendency for church planters to shape everything from scratch. Inventiveness, however, can create friction with preexisting programs. At some point, a church planter may find himself feeling restricted by something someone else took precious time to build *for him*. That person's ideas could save the church planter a lot of effort. Creative submission may release you from the need to concoct every element of church life.

> **Helpful Hint:** Denominational leaders are on your side. Their programs may not feel like the best fit, but their underlying motive is your success. Getting to know the leaders will help you calculate the freedom you have to innovate within boundaries. Building trust with them will lengthen the boundaries of that freedom.

Turn the Coach into a Champion

Every church planter needs a coach. You will unnerve someone in your denomination who sees himself as a keeper of the past. Whoever coaches you into your relationships with your denomination should also defend you when you cross such a person.

In my own life there was one man who defended my first church's efforts to plant our first daughter church. He was actually a keeper of the status quo, but he was also my direct contact with our movement. He and I had a strong, though sometimes confrontational, relationship. That relationship provided cover for me whenever my church stepped over the line. This "keeper of tradition" defended Hope Chapel's excursions beyond our boundaries. His willingness to protect and champion our sometimes upsetting ideas helped open our movement to the rush of church planting that it enjoys today.

Our first daughter church violated three very important rules that have since ceased to exist. The first was that we could not have two Foursquare churches in the same town. The second required pastors to graduate from a Bible college or seminary. The third rule was that the denomination planted churches; local churches did not.

That man, who so many saw as a traditionalist, championed our cause while others threw verbal stones. He not only provided protection for us, but he also turned our denomination into a church-planting movement.

Remember, denominational officials are your friends. Most will hold you in deep respect because they are a little intimidated by the task that you have chosen. You will find these people willing to work with you if you explain whatever difficulties you have with existing programs. Growing denominations always respect church planters as the cutting edge of leadership, development and innovation.

How Can Wealthy Patrons Help?

I have met several well-to-do people who wanted to support a new church out of their own pockets. This is a great idea because the relationship can be quite simple and often allows funding of ministries that might otherwise be overlooked. The downside is that business success does not always lead to spiritual understanding.

I know one well-meaning individual who recruited a young couple to move to a remote Pacific island where he had several business ventures. His idea was that they would begin a new church by discipling his employees. Their problems began just a few days after they moved to the new location. They did not understand their friend's business. They found it difficult to buy into his priorities. They began to sense needs within the community, not just in the company. Ministry success in those areas pulled them away from their original agreement. They soon crossed swords with their sole means of support. The venture failed; their friendship disintegrated. This young couple was left to finance their way home from a foreign country and begin life all over again. At this writing, they are rebuilding their shattered finances and hope to plant a new congregation with parent-church support.

In another situation a businessman had great insights and communication skills. But he did not understand mission philosophy and the importance of spiritual values as a driving force in a new church. He sought to superimpose unbiblical ideas on the fledgling congregation he helped start. His motives were fine; his methods were not. Had the church planters he sponsored worked out a mission philosophy before agreeing to work with him, they could have been successful. Unfortunately they had not.

I am not suggesting that you refuse to accept money from a patron. I am cautioning you and suggesting that you establish very firm parameters around the operation long before it begins. Folks with the financial horsepower to fund your mission will be strong-minded individuals. You need very clear parameters if you expect to work with them. You will never want to find yourself compromising some important spiritual principle because you owe something to somebody.

SHOULD YOU FUND YOUR OWN CHURCH PLANT?

As a church planter, you will make the greatest investment in this adventure. Your emotions, your spiritual well-being and the future of your family are all on the line. There are also times when personal savings and even debt may come into play.

When my wife and I planted the first Hope Chapel, we inherited an empty building and $600 from our denomination spread over four months. Our denomination was much smaller than it is now and had not yet developed a clear vision to plant churches. We invested the down payment we had saved for a home into the new church. It was our baby. We understood that we were drawing outside the lines and were willing to risk everything to finance it. I still remember the day when we spent our last cent. That was the day I *heard* God say, "I've taught you how to abase; now I will teach you to abound" (see Phil. 4:12, my paraphrase). Two days later, money began to flow freely from sources both inside and outside our church. We never borrowed money against credit cards, although I have heard of pastors who do. For us, only our personal savings were available to invest. Debt was not an option.

The one positive side to investing your own money in a church plant is the freedom you gain to ask your friends and family to give to the project. It is much easier for me to give money to a fund-raising campaign when the recipient is also making a sacrifice.

The obvious downside to this kind of thinking is that the money is not yours alone. It represents the future of your spouse and children. You should not use it if they oppose the idea. You should also beware of the idea of volunteer poverty as a condition to ministry. I do not believe that poverty is part of your calling. If God is really calling you to this adventure, He will provide enough so that your needs are met. Your children may not wear Nikes, but you will have food to eat and a roof over your heads.

Your Friends and Family Can Help

One way that people self-finance ministries is through the help of their family and friends. They solicit individuals who will guarantee support over a period of time. I see this as a means of self-financing, rather than relational support for the ministry. By this I mean the individual does not have the backing of a network of people and therefore is forced to raise money on his own. While useful, it sidesteps the ideal of churches birthing churches. Your friends and family help you financially, but they will not—and cannot—replace the kind of support you would receive from a parent church.

If you choose to raise money among family and friends, be sure to keep them apprised of the ministry situation. This goes beyond simple reports into actual financial accountability. Let them know what you are doing with the money. Let them know where your needs are. Treat them like partners in the venture. As you do, you will find that more money comes your way. In 2 Corinthians 8 and 9, the apostle Paul lays out three different concepts for raising money:

1. He shared his needs openly.
2. He allowed one group to know what another was doing for him.

3. He promised God's blessing upon those who part-
nered with him in the extension of the gospel.

Be sure that your fund-raising letters address all three. Let your
supporters know your needs. Allow your donors to know each
other, so everyone knows you have no secret sources of funding.
Announce your victories—give your supporters room to rejoice.

You Can Serve Bivocationally
Bivocational pastors are my heroes. They bring the gospel into the
community while bringing financial aid to their churches.
Because salary is such a large part of any budget, the bivocational
route should be an option for every potential pastor or staff member to at least explore. I will cover this more in a later chapter.

CHURCH PLANTER'S CHECKLIST

1. List and prioritize all available sources of funding,
   beginning with the most promising.
2. Identify any relational problems that might conceiv-
   ably occur with each funding source.
3. Note who you can communicate with now to prevent
   problems later.
4. Who should you ask about denominational expectations? On a scale of 1 to 10, how open and honest can
   you be with this person? If you cannot speak frankly,
   look for another contact.

PART 2

DESIGNING THE
New Church

CHAPTER 6

VALUES:
HOW SHOULD THEY DRIVE YOUR PLAN?

I grew up in the 1950s when men wore business suits to church. That dress code extended to little boys. For someone to come dressed in Levi's and tennis shoes meant that they were either very poor or quite disrespectful. However, one blue-jeans-wearing attendee taught me a great lesson.

Our church operated a bus ministry. Teams of adults would go door-to-door in poorer communities and invite young people to Sunday School. It was a great evangelistic outreach used by many churches for more than half a century, and it resulted in thousands of conversions. But not every member at my church was comfortable with all aspects of this outreach. One day I overheard a middle-aged woman complain about the way that a young man from the bus program was attired. She griped, "What's the matter with these bus kids? Doesn't this kid know he should not wear tennis shoes in God's house?"

This was a nice lady. She worked hard in several ministries at our church and was a prime mover in our Sunday School. She probably donated money to keep the bus ministry in operation. Her problem was the narrowness of her thinking. She apparently did not understand Jesus when He said that man looks at the outward appearance while God looks at the heart. She also did not recognize our church's stated value, which rejected dress as a criterion for admittance to our services.

The problem that she represented was not one of good versus evil, but one of a separation of values. I remember thinking that day about Jesus' story of the widow who gave her last penny to the Temple treasury in Jerusalem. This woman's comment drove the point of Jesus' parable deep into my heart. She so completely missed His message that I was forced to catch it. From that moment on, even to this day, I have had a deep commitment to bring the gospel to every person regardless of his or her outward appearance.

My understanding of the gospel and its core values causes me to want to evangelize gay people as much as straight people. It makes me care about rich people as much as the poor. It forces me to regard drug addicts with the same enthusiasm that I direct toward beautiful young children. Everyone, no matter how he or she looks or acts, needs to hear the gospel.

GRASP THE VALUE OF VALUES

When you set out to plant a new church, write out a values statement and display it as a blueprint and teaching tool. This is different from a vision statement and should reflect your basic worldview as it is influenced by the Scriptures. You should probably come up with 10 to 12 statements that will undergird decision making in your new church. A vision statement deals with goals; a values statement is a roadmap toward ethics and integrity.

Values Undergird Vision

Think about your personal values. What you deem important will lie at the center of every decision you make and will serve as the foundation of your vision. Any church you plant will stand upon the footprints of your personal values—values that have been gathered over a lifetime of observation, pain and success.

They influence everything you do. They are also *unique* to *you*. Although you work hard to base your decisions on Scripture, your views and choices are also a product of your personal experiences. Events like the one I described at the beginning of this chapter influence your judgment calls.

Helpful Hint: When you set out to craft a statement of values, stay away from the Internet. This exercise is not about amalgamating the values statements of the 10 largest churches in the country. It is about you and the kind of leader God wants you to be. You should fully embrace the idea of core values emanating from *your* view of the world.

I believe the Holy Spirit helps each person establish and build values. He controls the overall direction of your life, if not your responses to each situation. He speaks to your heart during times of crisis. Because of this, He is the coauthor of your values, as He is of your vision. He crafted you for the calling He has placed in your heart.

One reason values are so important is that you will attract people much like yourself. If your values add up to poor character, you will pastor a church with a mean spirit. If your values are lofty, your congregation will offer great service to the kingdom of God. Beyond the values you *unknowingly* display are those you *intentionally* bring into your life and ministry. The better your grip on your values, the more likely you will have a positive impact.

What Do You Think?

You should ask yourself: *What do I stand for in ministry? What issues are really important to me? Is evangelism a priority? Where do children fit into my view of the world? How about social justice? Do I care about the poor? What do I think of the AIDS epidemic? What of divorce and remarriage?*

Answers to these and other questions will define the church you plant.

What Events Shape Your Worldview?

Draw a simple time line to illustrate your life. Break it into sections built around your educational experiences. Start with the preschool years, then move to kindergarten, the primary grades, high school, college, postgraduate study and the school of hard knocks. Identify significant events (the use of pictures and symbols works well). Then catalogue the events in terms of values you acquired or reinforced at each level. You will find that your core values are a greater product of your experiences than you first thought.

What Is Your Core Value?

Another way to identify core values is to catch an end-goal perspective. Ask yourself, *What will I stand for at the end of my life?* Imagine your epitaph. Have you ever thought about what you would engrave on your own tombstone if given the opportunity. I have—I would write, "He was faithful." I believe this is the most important measure of my life. I hope that I live up to my roles, my gifts and the needs of God's kingdom. Scripture declares, "Moreover it is required in stewards, that a man be found faithful" (1 Cor. 4:2, *KJV*). This is the overriding value in my life. What is the predominant value in your life?

For me, faithfulness includes successfully planting lots of churches. This is because I have a strong sense of a God-given call to that task. It also means that I care for underprivileged people. I work at evangelizing homosexuals because I see the rest of the church avoiding them. I address marriage and family issues in otherwise healthy adults because families are coming apart in our community. I care for the addicted person because he is helpless without the power of the Holy Spirit. Above all, I give myself to my own family because, even though I am a pastor, they are my first priority. Some of the areas I have listed are unique to me because of my calling; others should apply to every pastor. The important thing is that you and I remain faithful to the end of our lives and that we accomplish all God hopes we will. What is not so important is to build the biggest church possible or to achieve fame among our peers. We should simply want to hear those words, "Well done, my good and faithful servant" (Matt. 25:21).

What Will "They" Say About You?

You should ask yourself, *What do I want people to say about the church I pastor?* Perhaps your enemies make the best judges on this question. They can be very descriptive and often succinct.

Hope Chapel was called "the hippie church" when we first began reaching street kids. Later we were "the bake-sale church" because we served coffee and donuts before others did. We have been known as "the church for poor people," but at the same time people accused us of being there only for the wealthy. I guess criticism at both ends of the financial spectrum means that we achieved balance. People from other churches have called us names because we do not judge young kids who come to church dressed like they would at a nightclub. Once we were accosted (one guy tried to physically take over the pulpit) when we focused on evangelism rather than attacked leaders in our community during a brouhaha over same-sex marriage. We had long taken the stand that Jesus died for those people and that befriending them with the gospel was our priority. We felt that it was important to stick to our values—and our newly redeemed friends—during this trying time. I have been called a "church-planting Nazi" because we continue to focus on the Great Commission. We have been labeled racists because we work hard to include everyone in our congregation, not just the dominant majority. All in all, our enemies describe us perhaps a little too colorfully, but very accurately.

You should wear these types of slanders by an enemy as backhanded compliments—like spiritual merit badges. The flattery of a friend (especially in a prepared introduction to a speech) is seldom to be trusted. Yet the words of an enemy usually contain a significant degree of truth. If you embrace them, you will not have to deal with bitterness *or* forgiveness. You can simply acknowledge that you are making a difference in the world and that someone took notice.

START WITH YOUR VISION

What does God want to happen to people in the town where you will serve? The answer to that question should summarize your vision.

We often ask, What does God want *me* to do? That is a self-centered question and will cause you to build a pastor-centered church. Asking God what he wants for the community will get your eyes off yourself and on the people who need to hear the gospel and to be touched by the ministry you will start. If you ask first about the community and then about your involvement in it, you will gain real focus for ministry.

Remember, vision comes through communication with God, not just by doing the numbers. Jack Hayford once wrote an article about vision where he claimed he had no goals.[1] In it he said he started with no written goals. But during prayer time, he received goals from the Lord. The objectives God gave were always bigger and more unique than those he would have manufactured through statistical analysis. You need good planning and you need to study demographics, yet you still need fresh vision from heaven.

Heavenly vision will include possibilities where humans see impossibilities. It will illuminate needs that you would otherwise overlook. Supernatural insight will cause you to see opportunity in every problem your town presents.

Determine the Feel of Your Church

Try to describe the ideal church. Use *feelings* in your description. The environment would be inviting to what kinds of people? Its campus would seem like what else besides a church? How should a person feel upon leaving a weekend celebration? Children's areas would have what kind of atmosphere? What emotions will people have after they have had contact with someone in one of your care ministries?

Feelings reflect your values. They also breed vision. Your church infrastructure and physical setup should reflect your feelings and those of your core team.

Take my church family as an example. Our church campus is intentionally more inviting to the people who live in our community than it is to tourists visiting Hawaii. Although we have a commanding view of the ocean and Kaneohe Bay, we center attention on a courtyard, which gives us a sheltered feel like that of an early California mission. Our weekend celebration is designed to leave people feeling equipped and uplifted (in that order). Those in our children's church are supposed to feel like they have spent a day in an amusement park, but we mix it with a school experience. Our care programs project feelings of hope to the hurting and of accomplishment to those who serve in our ministries.

I offer Hope Chapel as an example, but you should never try to merely copy any other church. Your ideas should reflect a lifetime of your own observations and experiences. The idea is to describe *your* ideal church. Give the Holy Spirit the opportunity to do something truly unique through you.

Find the Unmet Needs

When I began ministry, I was challenged by an older pastor to "Find a need and fill it!" His advice kept me ministering on the cutting edge of societal change. It also helped me see what the Lord sees in terms of human need. Salvation is more than numbers of people joining a church. It is the process of rescue from the dregs of sin. By looking for need, rather than at what others had done, I continue to discover emerging needs in an ever-changing world.

Meeting unmet needs will keep you relevant. It will also insure continued success in ministry. Church growth can become a game for clones and copycats. Many leaders use business models and build churches around the recent success of others. Unfortunately, they usually introduce a market-based competition for the already saved. Evangelism always means fishing in the deep waters of human need. Keep recognizing need and you will *always* have difficulty dragging into your boat the heavy nets that teem with your catch.

DISCOVER THE BIBLICAL PURPOSE FOR YOUR CHURCH

Purpose is the twine you use to tie your values and vision together. Your values are unique to you. Your vision will be for a church unlike any other in a community unlike any other. But your purpose should approximate that of every other church: equipping people to take God's love to the ends of Earth.

Think about it. Scripture actually binds the purpose for your ministry to the word "equip." As a pastor, you are called to equip God's people to do the work of ministry (see Eph. 4:11-13). Jesus also gave you an end goal. Your church is to help evangelize the entire world in a substantial way (see Matt. 28:18-20). Whatever else you do—your church must grow from these intertwining statements of purpose. Your job is to equip the people. Theirs is to teach all men everywhere to walk in obedience to Christ.

People do not join Hope Chapel; they join Team Hope, where every member is expected to have a ministry.[2] We are more than a little fanatical about this and feel we have to be. Otherwise busy people will nearly always choose a spectator's role. Our goal is 100 percent participation in ministry. We teach our newcomers this value and together we execute our vision—all because of our purpose.

Pull It All Together

A good exercise for wedding vision to values is to make a list of every element of church life that you can dream up. Look at each item on your list through the prism of these questions: How could this activity better fit my own ministry values? How does this activity fit into God's revealed plan for the people of this town? Is there a better way to accomplish the purpose behind this activity? Write the answers to these questions in your notebook. They are the beginning of your business or church-planting plan. It is from them that most of what you do during the first year of operation will grow.

Keep your eyes open. If your methods are unorthodox, you will take a little flak for your decisions. There will always be people who want you to fall in with the rest of the herd.

You should be able to defend your ideas biblically and from a perspective of human need. Trying to maintain church tradition should be the last of your worries as you launch your new venture. You do, however, owe it to both your critics and your followers to document your plans and your reasons for undertaking them. An unwritten plan is no plan at all. The goal of this book is to get you to write down your plan, which includes your vision, your core values and the other elements I have noted.

Helpful Hint: God is not calling *every* person you meet to participate in your new church. There will be many people who visit, and even hang around awhile, who can't or won't hear your voice as the shepherd's.

Furthermore, communication with your congregation and supporters should not only include what you plan to do but also why you are doing it. As you continue to write your plans, train yourself to describe your new church in *three minutes* with a heavy emphasis on why you are different from the other congregations in your community. A short little speech can turn critics into visionaries. You *will* be challenged—make it an opportunity.

Every church should be a little different from all others. The pastor's personality will color that difference as will the particular neighborhood and leadership team. Vision, values and application will differ from church to church and pastor to pastor. But it is not enough just to be different, you also need a good reason why you have chosen to be different and how being different will have an impact for the gospel. Note these reasons in your journal.

Finally, try to write a statement of purpose and a statement of mission. Write out why your church will exist, in 15 words or fewer. This is your statement of purpose. It should be a short summary of your values. Publish it on everything you print from T-shirts to church bulletins.

Also, using fewer than 50 words, delineate what you will accomplish in the first decade. This is your overall vision turned into a highly repeatable mission statement. For Hope Chapel, our mission was to "Plant enough churches to include 1 percent of the population of Hawaii in attendance in the first 10 years." Today we list local, national and worldwide goals. The important thing is not that your purpose and mission statements parallel someone else's, but that you have them in place and that they rest on your values the way a building rests on its foundation.

CHURCH PLANTER'S CHECKLIST

1. Draw a time line representing your life. Identify value-changing moments. Name the values you gleaned from each of them.
2. What words would you like written on your tombstone? Why?
3. What would you want an enemy to say about the church you will soon plant?
4. List three things you believe God wants to happen in the town where you will serve. Next to each, write a short paragraph describing how your church could help them happen.
5. Write two pages that describe the perfect church—focus on feelings.
6. Write a statement of purpose in 15 words or fewer.
7. List reasonable one- and five-year goals for your church.

Notes

1. Jack W. Hayford, "Why I Don't Set Goals," *Leadership* (Winter 1984), p. 46.
2. Ralph Moore, *Let Go of the Ring* (Honolulu, HI: Straight Street Publications, 1993), pp. 57-58.

CHAPTER 7

TEAM:
WHO WILL PARTNER WITH YOU?

When I first embraced the vision of planting a new church in Kaneohe, Hawaii, I told one friend my secret. Aaron Suzuki was a surfing buddy. He also spent many hours teaching me how to keep my old British sports cars running. Our friendship was rooted in the Lord, but was not oriented toward ministry or the church. We were just good friends.

I shared my thoughts with Aaron even before I told my wife. I did not want to scare her if this was just another of my wild goose chases. I figured Aaron would help me sort out my thoughts and feelings. He surprised me by telling me that he had for some time felt called into ministry, specifically ministry in

Hawaii where he had grown up. If I went, he would be interested in bringing his wife and coming along for the adventure. A prayer team was born that evening. The next night we got our wives together and told them what we were thinking. Both spouses felt this was from the Lord.

ASSEMBLE A STRONG CHURCH-PLANTING TEAM

Church planting is a team process. Jesus assembled a team to launch the church in Jerusalem. Paul used and promoted teams during his missionary travels. Today's successful church planters are almost always team builders. Individuals or single family units have planted churches, but not often and always with much difficulty.

If you want to plant a church, you need a team. If you want to have a successful church plant, then you need to assemble, build and lead a cohesive unit that performs to its potential. In this chapter, I lay out some principles and give practical tips on how you can begin and proceed along the team-building process.

Pray with Close Friends

Everywhere I go I see potential. Every vacation and each ministry trip leaves me feeling frustrated that I cannot move somewhere else and plant another church. The needs are overwhelming, the opportunities endless. Launching churches from a strong base is the best way to meet these opportunities. That is what my wife always tells me. Nonetheless, I always wish I could run off and start something new. This is why I need to remain in close contact with a few good friends who are not afraid to take the wind out of my sails.

When my friends embraced the idea of a move from Southern California to Hawaii, I began to see beyond my own pipe dreams and into the work of the Spirit. Without their prayers and wisdom

I am not sure what would have happened. All I can conclude is that if anyone plans to start a new church, they had better have a group of honest friends praying through all the false starts, opposition and unexpected hurdles.

A group of people who pray is the foundation of a core ministry team. Your prayer partners may or may not move to the new location with you. Their job is to make sure you get there in one piece.

Win Parent-Church Permission

One of the most important issues you will face is that of winning permission from your parent church. You need to approach the parent church leadership team in a way that reinforces your relationship with it.

A strong parent church ensures success. Initial communication over your plan is a matter of urgent prayer. You need to invest time on your knees *before* you approach the leaders of your mother church. If the potential parent-church leadership misunderstands your motives, you could face a disaster. Make this relationship work well, and you are off to the races. Threaten the parent church with fears of division or suspicion of rebellion, and you are dead at the starting line.

Helpful Hint: Do not even think about planting a church without the involvement of a parent church. From time to time I meet people who think they are lone ranger Christians. When one of them tries to plant a church it most often results in a disaster, ranging from simply a lack of ministry skills to cultlike behavior. If you are not currently serving in a local congregation, you need to make some changes. This advice also applies to anyone with parachurch experience. Churches beget churches and pastors beget pastors.

Extend Spiritual Lifelines

You should approach the leadership team of the parent church with an attitude of thanksgiving for their investment in your life and family. It is that investment that you will now try to extend into a new community via a church plant. You may do something radically different in form from the parent church, but make clear that the spark of life will come from it as your own life came from a relationship between your parents.

You might want to write a letter that defines your plan and back it up with verbal communication. In your letter you will want to (1) state your appreciation for all you have received from the church, (2) delineate your vision in very simple terms (for example: "To start a new church in such-and-such community as a direct spiritual offspring of our church"), and (3) ask for permission to pursue the project.

Do not go into the details, particularly timetables. That information will arise when you are questioned further about your idea. The major purpose of the first meeting (or communication) is to put the idea on the table in submission to your elders. I have done this twice. Both times I was met with loving support. In the first instance the question immediately arose "How are we going to get through summer camp if you plant a church?" The second time I had to make this kind of request, the leadership team immediately worried about who would take my place. In both situations, there were easy solutions to the problems. By surrendering my heart to God at the outset, the question "To plant or not to plant?" never became a big deal.

Do Not Let Rumors Start

If you choose to plant within driving distance of your parent church, you risk the perception that your move is a church split. To forestall such fears, be sure that everyone you speak with knows your personal loyalty to the church you are leaving. Also, be sure that you communicate the needs of unreached people in your new location. Be certain that you define your core team as specially called individuals who will help birth the new church. Make known that coming with you to plant a new church is their *calling*, not a random idea or an expression of frustration against the parent church.

When we began the church-planting process, we called our core team a gestation group. This unwieldy term demanded definition every time we used it. Defining and redefining the term kept the idea of spiritual birth in everyone's minds. As a result, we never had any lingering fears of rebellion or disunity.

Helpful Hint: If you are disguising a church split as a church plant, then you can expect God's judgment rather than His blessing.

Build Your Team(s)

When I moved from California to Hawaii, the Lord built two core teams. We did not realize it until after we moved. But our unified team that started had two distinct functions. One group was to actually make the move. The other was in place to keep our prayer needs before the parent church once we were gone. From the outset, however, we all thought we were moving. God supernaturally provided employment and housing opportunities for about half of the people involved. He just as actively shut doors for the others. His wishes became apparent and we realized that there is a prayer-support role in church planting. This is much like those roles held by Simeon, Manaen or Lucius of Cyrene among the church planters in Antioch (see Acts 13:1).

Recruit Team Members

Do not put a lot of effort into recruiting a church-planting team. Let the Holy Spirit bring members to you. He will do this in two ways. First, He will speak to you during times of prayer. He will show you the people He has marked out as your partners in ministry. Go ask these people to pray about joining you in this venture. Second, He will draw people around you through word of mouth. There will be people you barely know who will come as a result of the Spirit's nudging. One man sat in our church for six years without ever becoming directly involved in ministry. When Guy Kapeliela announced that he was planting a church six miles away in Olomana, this man became enthused. He and his wife offered to join the core team. Today, he has left his successful business and serves as the church administrator. None of us could have recruited him because none of us knew him.

God will send people, and He picks the right ones. I have watched prospective pastors try to recruit people because they thought they were big givers (usually they were not). Some have tried to recruit the next wave of church planters. That is unwise. It is usually best that the mother church continues to mentor them and send them out a year or two later with financial resources that a young church might not be able to provide. One guy tried to recruit the spouse of one of our brightest young staff members. He had planned on asking this staff member to come along also—but with no salary. Human effort is unnecessary and hurtful compared with asking the Lord of the harvest to pull together a team of His choosing. Again, do not panic—the Lord will meet your needs if you put your trust in Him.

Pastor and Disciple Your Core Team

At Hope Chapel, we begin our core-team meetings five months before the launch date of a new church. There is no special reason for five months. We did it that way during an early church plant and found that it works well. During this time the new pastor becomes the primary pastor to his team members and disciples them toward the founding of the new church. The core team is foundational to everything that follows. It is literally the fetus of the unborn church. Your job during this time is to build your values, vision and purpose into each team member. You should become their pastor in that they begin to see you as the spiritual leader in their life. You should be their discipler, too. During this time, build in your team members a new paradigm for ministry in a new setting.

You should have regular meetings, and perhaps you can even eat together. Meeting on Sunday afternoons makes it easy for new team members to show up. Sharing a meal can build a party atmosphere around the birth of the new church. The joy of great fellowship will flood over into planning sessions and the culture of the new congregation. After all, a birth is something we all celebrate.

Work with your team to build a plan using this book or a similar tool. Let the book take you through the step-by-step process of moving people from *membership* in one spiritual household into *leadership* in one yet to be created. Give them your opinion about what I have written in this book. You are the leader, and your ideas must prevail.

> **Helpful Hint:** Give the members of your core team weekly reading assignments. Ask each member to copy meaningful quotes and insights into a journal. Be sure they leave space to write more during your time together.

Allow lots of time for discussion and mutual daydreaming. Let the new church *emerge* from your discussions. You will soon have dozens of fresh ideas about how to do ministry. As new ideas emerge, make plans. As your plans grow, assign responsibilities. Match people with the ministries or tasks for which they show the most passion. Passion is epidemic when launching a new congregation. Let training and other preparation take a backseat to it. But be sure, when you assign responsibility for a task, you also give the person authority to recruit onto their team others of like passion.

Log the shape of your new church on a very fluid organizational chart. One that I like is found in Wayne Cordeiro's book *Doing Church as a Team*.[1] His idea of fractal leadership (the inspiration of which he credits to Youth With a Mission's Loren Cunningham) allows the church to take shape around passion and fruitfulness. It also presses the task of recruitment away from centralized leadership and toward the people actually doing the ministry.

Turn Workers into Disciple Makers

Teach the people on your core team that they are to make disciples within the new church as soon as it is born. This means that they should try to replace themselves in their ministry positions within the first six to nine months. It will be easier for them to discover a new ministry opportunity than for someone new to the church. They are to disciple a replacement, move out of the way, find a new need and fill it. This practice helps you to turn every productive team member into a multiplier of workers. The ministry will grow more quickly if lots of people are recruiting and training others. Placing each new person into ministry causes the church to resemble Peter's model. He said the church was made of living stones fitted together into a spiritual building (see 1 Pet. 2:5). Your new church will look a lot like a loose pile of rocks from the beginning. Your core team must connect them together into this building.

Practice Succession Management

If you plan ahead to graduate leaders into new positions as I have described above you will be paving the way toward what I call "succession management." The idea here is for every person to recruit two or three apprentices to help with his or her task. The assistant then succeeds the leader when that person is ill, on vacation or moves on to another task. Most people have a pool of roughly 20 friends from which they can draw. If one person recruits for an entire department, his or her recruiting pool is sorely pressed and recruitment becomes a burden. If each person on the team is made a recruiter, the task spreads over many of these pools of talent. This approach reduces the load of responsibility at every level. Because recruitment works through relationships, ministry tasks take on an air of friendship and joy. Most importantly, the church explodes with expansion and growth.

Create an Escape Clause

About half of the people who show up your first weekend will not be with you six months later. Many will come from other churches, including the parent congregation. Many of these will discover that you do not match their idea of the ideal pastor. You should make it easy for them to exit with grace and dignity.

Provide a back door from the first day. Ask your core team to sign on for a three- or six-month commitment. A commitment provides predictability. The short duration will keep an unhappy person in place just long enough for them to recruit a replacement. It will also keep their spirits up toward the project, since they know they have a way out.

Our experience at Hope Chapel shows us that many people who make the short-term commitment will work out their uncomfortable feelings toward the end of their term and decide to stay for the long haul. However, experience also teaches that long-term or indefinite commitments cause people to begin criticizing leadership in order to justify leaving. When people have this kind of agenda, it has a demoralizing effect on others in the church. Moreover, the unhappy person seldom returns to the parent church because he or she is embarrassed over his or her negative actions and attitude. A back door allows those who leave to return to the parent church, often with valuable information for the next church planters. They become an information resource for the leaders who will eventually send out another team.

Give Back to Your Parent Church

You should always attempt to give something back to your parent church. This gift can come in the form of members you send back with knowledge, a symbolic trophy or a financial gift toward a building fund. Whatever it is, you should give *something*. Giving binds hearts in partnership. Sometimes a new church will think its new ways are superior to the traditions of the congregation that birthed it. Leaders in the parent church may question the methods of the newly planted church or may doubt its choice of leaders. Giving a gift has a way of joining hearts when points of view differ.

Remember your heritage and reinforce it. You are a product of your parent church. Make them proud of you—not just proud of your numbers, but proud of your leadership. Make them proud that you carry their torch into a new community. Doing so will stimulate you and them to love and to do good works.

BUILD UPON A BIBLE-STUDY GROUP OR FAILED CHURCH PLANT

Once in a while an uncommon opportunity presents itself. This is the chance to build a church around an existing group of people. Perhaps the group is a home Bible study in a new community that decides it wants to become a church. Maybe the church you get called to plant will actually be a congregation that has shrunk to a handful of people. In either case, you will face different problems than the pastor who starts with nothing. Your priority is to mold a philosophy of ministry in the hearts of your people.

An existing network of people provides some very attractive shortcuts to a new church. These groups usually have amassed some money as well as an income stream. They have leadership infrastructure. And they represent a common desire to grow a church.

However, an existing network may conceal hidden reefs that could sink your ship as well. They will have no unified vision as to the values and style of the new congregation. Worse yet, some may want to replicate the past on a larger scale. There may be people who wanted your job but were overruled by their friends. They may still want the job and might compete with you for it. There may be someone who wants his brother-in-law as pastor instead of you.

You should approach an offer to pastor an existing group with a very soft touch. Do not set your heart on the job. Be very strong about the terms of your commitment and very soft toward the decision to move forward. Lay out your values and philosophy of ministry in the strongest terms possible. Be sure you specify what is nonnegotiable. Then back off and let the group make the hiring decision without any lobbying on your part. This will force them either to buy into your values or to reject you as their pastor. Doing so will save everyone boatloads of grief later on.

If you do take the job, be quick to change *nothing*. I learned this wisdom from a woman named Henrietta Mears. She was the driving force behind the success of Hollywood Presbyterian Church in the 1940s and 1950s. When first hired to direct the Christian education ministry of the church, she announced that she would change nothing for the first six months. This was out of respect for the wonderful job everyone was doing. Of course, she found herself flooded with notices of what needed change. She spent those first six months teaching values to leaders. They fed the values back as portents of change. She spent the next few years helping them implement *their* ideas. She earned the right to lead by respecting the people she worked with. Under her influence, the church grew from a few hundred people to many thousands. During those years, Miss Mears established important ministries, including Gospel Light Publications, Forest Home Christian Conference Center and GLINT—an international Christian publisher. Her influence was strongly felt in the lives of Bill Bright and Billy Graham.[2]

One of my friends recently became the pastor of an existing small church. He went to visit a congregation of 45 people who chose to make him their pastor. On his first Sunday in the pulpit, there were 176 people present, with most of the new folks coming from our congregation 20 miles away. Within months that group had doubled in size. He was forced to build a support unit of differing individuals with different values into one solid group.

His plan was to run the church without changing anything run on Sunday mornings for the first three months. During that time he built a leadership core by teaching his values on Sunday afternoons. He shaped these people into a viable congregation within a matter of weeks. He did struggle with a couple of people from the preexisting group who felt threatened by the rapid growth. But by hailing to their *shared value* of evangelism, my friend helped these faithful people choose to stay and to weather the growth they had long prayed over.

Mutual understanding *before* the project ever gets off the ground is the first key to success with an existing network. Respect for their past is the second. Moreover, a value-building process must parallel or precede rapid growth.

CHURCH PLANTER'S CHECKLIST

1. Do you have a couple of praying friends who are committed to your project? Name them.
2. Do you have parent-church permission and backing for this venture? If not, sketch out a letter introducing the idea and ask for the blessing you need.
3. Are you praying for the Lord to help you put together a team, or are you recruiting willy-nilly? How can you improve in this area?
4. In five sentences write out an escape clause you can give to people who will go with you to start a new church.

Notes

1. Wayne Cordeiro, *Doing Church as a Team* (Ventura, CA: Regal Books, 2001), p. 178.
2. Earl O. Roe, ed., *Dream Big: The Henrietta Mears Story* (Ventura, CA: Regal Books, 1990), pp. 336–354.

CHAPTER 8

PROPOSAL:
WHAT SHOULD YOU CONSIDER BEFORE ASKING FOR MONEY?

I have met pastors who hate writing budgets. I love the process. When I was in high school I took a personal business class. The teacher asked the class to plan a seven-day vacation by automobile to anywhere we wanted to go. I drew an elaborate plan for a surfing trip from Portland, Oregon (where I lived), to Los Angeles. I calculated the costs and even scheduled my rest stops and meal times. I got a C on the project because the teacher thought seven days was not enough time for such a long journey. Later, I made the trip on a four-day weekend. Proving the teacher wrong was half the fun; proving my schedule and budget was workable was the other half.

Budgets are wonderful because they function as a schedule and a road map to what would otherwise be an unattainable future. Your budget is your friend. The more time you put into the relationship, the more you will get out of it. The more attention you give to the details, the less likely you are to come up short and begging once the operation is under way.

CREATE OPPORTUNITY AND OPERATIONS BUDGETS

You really need two budgets. One is an opportunity budget; the other is for operational costs. They are different in function, and you should approach them from vastly different angles.

The operations budget enables you to plan and control recurring ministry costs. You want to limit these costs to the minimum needed in each area. An opportunity budget encompasses one-time opportunities, such as your first public meeting or an initial advertising campaign. This is the place where you *want* to spend money and lots of it. Your goal is to hold operating costs down so you have lots of money to spend on opportunities. If you do this well ultimately you will need to spend even more on operations, the size of which will increase as you progress.

A Look at What Is in Each Budget
An opportunity budget should include the following expenses:

1. Outreach
2. Core-team meetings
3. Opening-day functions
4. Banners, signs and information center

5. A stationery package
6. Sound system
7. TV projection system
8. Chairs and other furniture for worship celebration
9. Equipment for children's ministry
10. Advertisement and promotion
11. An adequate communication system to operate the church as a team of volunteers, including cell phones, e-mail software and computers

Your operations package should encompass the following costs:

1. Pastor's salary (we pay a planting pastor a full-time salary if he has been serving full-time on our staff. Otherwise he plants as a bivocational pastor)
2. Support staff that you decide to pay (usually part-time)
3. Rent for your meeting place
4. Office rents if you incur them
5. Printing costs
6. Telephone, Internet access and utilities
7. Insurance
8. A benefits package for the pastor if he is paid by the church

Make Sure Your Priorities Are Right
The first time Hope Chapel sent someone out to start a church, we equipped the pastor with 25 people and $3,000. The pastor was bivocational, making more money from his secular job than I was from my employment in the mother church. The church met in a home for the first few months and then in a rented community center. They functioned without

an office for more than a year. All they had to deal with was an opportunity budget. They spent all the money on outreach. The church grew quickly and was able to fund operations from the offerings of the congregation. They grew to nearly 500 members, planted two daughter churches and built a ranch for troubled teens within their first six years. The wisdom of their plan was that they focused their resources entirely on opportunity without generating operational costs until absolutely necessary.

I started the first Hope Chapel 15 months before we planted our first daughter church. We did not have to pay rent, but we were still responsible for utilities, yard service, building maintenance and the like. I was also determined to work full time in ministry. In our situation, nearly every penny went to operations. There was very little left over for outreach during those exciting days when everything we did was brand new.

The outreach we managed to pull off was due to the generosity of an outsider. W. Clement Stone, a man we never met, gave us money to distribute large numbers of David Wilkerson's book *The Cross and the Switchblade* at no cost. This book offered a spiritual remedy to the fledgling drug epidemic. Without Stone's help, we would have stalled into a tiny pool of operational expenses and few people. Because I did not understand the difference between opportunity and outreach at the time, we almost squandered our future.

You Can Keep Costs Down

First-time church planters often mistake ministry hardware for symbols of success. I regularly battle with people who would rather spend money on office space than advertising space in the newspaper. At Hope Chapel, we look for ways to keep our overhead down. Our strategy is to build *virtual* offices. We take advantage of the best communications technology available to link key volunteers. Computers and cell phones are our friends if we use them well. E-mail and the Internet work just as well, if not better, than some traditional methods of organization and communication.

At Hope Chapel, we would rather tap technology than spend 10 times the money on office space. When we need to meet face-to-face, we can always find a coffee shop. There are several we use regularly as a ministry base, and the proprietors do not mind at all. We generate business for them and save ourselves thousands of dollars at the same time.

Technology and advertising are prime examples of opportunity investments. These usually, although not always, occur as one-time expenses. Announcing your presence in the community through intense advertising is a one-time opportunity. An ongoing presence in the newspaper or yellow pages, however, is a maintenance cost; it is operational.

USE YOUR BUDGET AS A FUND-RAISING TOOL

Some people contend that planning is not spiritual. They expect the Lord to lead them but do not want to spend much time in thought or prayer. For these people budgets and calendars seem like needless restrictions or "tools of the flesh." Such a view causes some people to overlook powerful equipment for building momentum and raising money. A budget is simply a calendar with event costs estimated in detail. The calendar gives you momentum because every event represents a goal, and people get excited about challenging goals. The representation of cost creates a tangible need, which can stimulate visionary people to invest large sums of money.

Your dream church journal is the foundation for your calendar and budget. As your ideas grow, begin to assemble a calendar. Separate must-hit target dates from can-do events. Allow lots of room for input from your growing core team. Put everything on paper.

As your calendar grows, build a simple budget around your targets. When will you buy what hardware? Which advertising tools will you use on what days and how much will they cost? Where will you meet? On which date will you start paying rent? Which personnel costs will you assume on which dates? This may be a long list, but you need as much detail as you can get.

Circulate each revision of your budget among your core-team members and prayer supporters. Treat it as a living document until it becomes finalized (usually upon negotiating a final version with parent-church leaders or denominational officials). Each generation of the budget carries more power to excite people about your project and puts them in a mind-set to support the new church.

Talk about your plans wherever you go. You will be surprised how much money you will generate just by communicating your needs through everyday conversations. One way you can do this is by building a very simple website for the new church. Post your statement of purposes, values and vision as well as your calendar and budget so that people can spy out the land from their desktops. The Internet will move you beyond fund-raising into inciting people to join your team. The website can allow your team members to e-mail data to their friends, inviting them to join you.

As your budget comes closer to finality, publish it on paper in a nice graphic format, so you can distribute it at any meetings where you are called upon to explain it. Keep it simple. Tuck an offering envelope in the back of the package to make it easier for individuals to contribute. This is just one way that your budget actually becomes a fund-raising tool.

Pool Your Resources

In 53 B.C., Cyrus the king of Persia sent a ragtag band of Jews home to Judah. They were to rebuild the Temple of the Lord in Jerusalem. You might call their project a church plant since seven decades earlier the Temple had been destroyed and worship had been cut off.

A man named Ezra assumed the role of church planter. Cyrus and Ezra utilized three separate funding sources besides the personal contributions of time and money made by the planting team. He received support from the Jewish survivors in Diaspora, King Cyrus's own gifts and the loot taken from the Temple (see Ezra 1—2).

Modern church planters usually operate in a similar fashion, using funds from several pools. The Scriptures do not say much about Ezra's skill at planning or budgeting. We just know that he was successful at pulling together the efforts of various sectors of the populace and that he built the Temple within the allotted time. Your goal, as a church planter, is to emulate his success.

You will draw money from at least five resources.

1. Your parent church
2. Your denomination
3. The core team
4. Personal acquaintances, including family and friends
5. The new congregation

You need to communicate your needs to each of these pools. Face-to-face visits work best, although at some point you will have to resort to letters and e-mail.

Devise a Fund-Raising Plan

Denominations usually have a preset financial package for church planters. These setups seldom distinguish between

opportunity and operational budgets. If you have denominational funds available to you, try to channel them into advertising and outreach.

Your parent church and acquaintances will usually prefer to
give toward the purchase of material things. They can easily
focus on the need for computers or a sound system. An individual might be challenged to buy chairs in lots of 10. A small
church may take a special offering for a video projector.

At some point before the first service, core-team members
should redirect their tithes to the new church. At Hope Chapel,
we ask them to begin five months before the launch date. This
process weans the parent church from the offerings supplied by
the core team. It also generates among core-team members a
sense of ownership over both the income and expenses of the
new church.

However, keep in mind that all income support from outside
sources is short-term. Those funds are gifts, not entitlements.
Ultimately, the new congregation will carry the expenses of the
church plant. They will support it for several generations.

At Hope Chapel, our goal is always to get the new congregation to embrace the financial responsibility for their own future.
This is why we underwrite them only through the sixth month
of existence. Our assumption is that long-term support breeds
dependency and feelings of entitlement. I have spoken with pastors who enjoyed rich subsidies and then felt shortchanged
when those funds were finally cut off and they had to face full
financial responsibility. I believe that a practice of short-lived,
predictable and diminishing support helps produce independent and responsible daughter-church leaders.

In our situation, once we agree to an opportunity budget, we
find a way to fund it. When we have built an operations budget
we pool our resources (denominational and outside gifts,
parent-church offerings and core-team tithes) to fund 100 per-

cent of the first month's cost. The daughter church keeps whatever offerings come in. The second month, we provide 90 percent of the operational budget. The third month, this drops to 80 percent and decreases accordingly. All funding from the parent church ceases after the sixth month. Using this system, we have never had a congregation that could not stand on its own once the financial support ceased. We have also heard very few complaints that we give too little.

By front-loading support for opportunities during the first few months, we insure that the new church can operate with quality from the first weekend. By reducing the support each month, we put the new congregation on notice that it will only succeed if its pastor preaches on tithes and offerings and if the people heed his words. I equip young pastors with teaching tapes on these subjects. I also do my best to encourage church planters to talk frankly about the need for their people to obey God in this crucial area.

God offers support to churches. He promises to "supply all your needs from his glorious riches, which have been given to us in Christ Jesus" (Phil. 4:19). As a church planter, you need to pray and you need to teach people to give and to be careful stewards of their money. You also need thoughtful planning and communication of need. When all these elements come together, you can expect to lead a prosperous congregation where "God will generously provide all you need. Then you will always have everything you need and plenty left over to share with others" (2 Cor. 9:8).

CHURCH PLANTER'S CHECKLIST

1. Build a time line covering 18 months, beginning with a date six months prior to a church plant and advancing one year into the life of the church.
2. Attach costs to the above time line.
3. Separate your costs into two columns—one is for opportunities; the other demarcates operations.
4. Try to find creative ways to shift dollars from operations to opportunity.
5. Set a target date for operating without any additional support, for both operational and opportunity budgets.
6. Identify all funding sources available to you, and list ideas for how to best communicate with each of them.
7. Begin praying with friends for the income this project will require.

CHAPTER 9

SALARY:
SHOULD YOU BE A BIVOCATIONAL PASTOR?

In two consecutive years, drunk-driving accidents took the lives of several high school students in the village of Kahuku, Hawaii. In response, Walter Santiago decided to plant a church. He was an unlikely candidate for the task because he had been a Christian for only two years. But he felt impressed by the Holy Spirit that a new congregation, targeted toward young people, could meet the growing spiritual needs in the tragedy-scarred small town.

Walter had grown up in Kahuku and had been *the* star athlete on a conference champion football team. During the years the accidents occurred, he was a popular football coach at the high school. His stature in the community gave him inroads to the hearts of the townspeople.

Walter's congregation began as a high school Bible study, but it grew rapidly and now includes about 10 percent of the townspeople. He started as a bivocational pastor because there was little money available for his salary and few people wanted to support such a young believer in ministry. However, once the congregation grew, the church board had enough funds to pay a salary and requested he quit his secular job.

Tom McCarthy also felt a call to pastor. A layman, he was the backup preacher in my first church. The people loved him, and many speculated that he would assume my job when I moved to Hawaii. God had other plans. Tom, a gynecologist and part-time professor at UCLA, eventually moved to Santa Rosa, California, and purchased an existing medical practice. When he first arrived in Santa Rosa, he taught an adult Sunday School class in a mainline denominational church. Then, with the backing of his pastor and of Zac Nazarian, who had taken my place in Southern California, Tom planted a Hope Chapel. He maintained his medical practice, investing just 10 hours a week in the church. With the help of hired staff he grew the congregation to more than 1,000 regular attendees. Eventually the combination of church and medicine demanded too much time. Tom handed the church off to another pastor. Nonetheless, he knows that he is a gifted leader and church planter and, as I write, he is contemplating planting yet another congregation. He feels that his position in the community uniquely positions him to multiply churches.

Tom had both denominational and parent-church backing. He built a core team of strong tithers. Yet he chose bivocational ministry. He did this *not* because the church lacked funds, but because the bivocational approach *fit* his needs and life situation.

We should not let church multiplication slow because of a lack of funding—yet it happens too often. We need more people like

Walter and Tom. Neither man let work or money get in the way.

I was in Europe to teach at church-planting seminars when I met with pastors from Holland, France, Germany and Switzerland. Leaders from each of these countries had great stories about bivocational, church-planting pastors. But the Dutch examples stood out. The group I was with works exclusively with bivocational planters. They have started 45 churches in just 20 years. The pastor of the host church is an attorney and seasoned pastor of 500 people who, for many years, simultaneously maintained his law practice. His disciples are engineers and businessmen who work at their professions while they launch new congregations.

There will always be communities that have a difficult time supporting a full-time pastor and pastors who can better support their families with income from a secular job. These are solid reasons for a church planter to be bivocational.

Whatever the reason, you should at least look at every option available to you including a bivocational approach to finances. The purpose of this chapter is to help you determine whether or not a similar situation would work best for you. You can look at it this way: If you need a dump truck, a moped will never meet your needs. But if you need a moped, a dump truck will not help you either. Some jobs require one and then the other as time passes. You must discern and use the tool that is appropriate in your situation.

THE BIBLE SUPPORTS BIVOCATIONAL PASTORS

Examples of bivocational ministry in the Bible range from prophets such as Amos the fig farmer to Paul the tentmaker. Their numbers include Daniel the prime minister to Peter the fisherman.

The apostles were flexible regarding financial support. At one point, Paul argued forcefully that a pastor should be paid for service. He wrote, "The Lord gave orders that those who preach the Good News should be supported by those who benefit from it" (1 Cor. 9:14). Another time, in his letter to the church at Philippi, he embraced the idea of long-distance support for missionaries (see Phil. 4:10,14-18). But, in his final charge to the Ephesian elders, he also heartily backed bivocational ministry: "You know that these hands of mine have worked to pay my own way, and I have even supplied the needs of those who were with me. And I have been a constant example of how you can help the poor by working hard" (Acts 20:34-35).

Like Paul, I am not making a case for any single means of support. The idea is to discover what works best in your unique situation.

WE NEED MORE CHURCHES

In order to evangelize the world and make disciples of every person we need more churches. Larger congregations are not the answer. This is because it is a lot easier to teach several persons to pastor medium-sized churches than to teach one individual how to build a large one. Yet Western culture and tradition lean toward the larger church as the answer.

The North American church paradigm seems wired *against* the rapid multiplication of churches. At its core are three major impediments to the rapid multiplication of the church. Each roadblock is a useful tool, yet each comes with a price tag that is often out of reach or difficult to pay.

The costs that stand in our way include the following:

1. Required seminary training for pastors
2. A dedicated building for church services
3. Full-time remuneration for pastors

All three demand sizeable financial resources.

The first two on this list actually take time and focus away from evangelism and discipleship. Because time and money are tight, all three rob our ability to evangelize and plant churches aggressively.

Train Your Pastors Locally

Fortunately, the times are changing. Tradition is slowly bending. Churches everywhere are beginning to train laypeople to become staff members, and they are using biblical tools of discipleship to do this. Over time it is only natural that many of these disciples will launch new churches. Many will become senior pastors whose only training came from their parent church.

Many churches that train their own church planters have had negative experiences when they have sent prospective leaders off to seminary. Hope Chapel serves as an example. Early in my ministry I sent three pastoral prospects to local seminaries. All three immediately stopped doing any ministry in the church because of the time and energy demands of their study load. Although each graduated on schedule, only one reentered ministry. One was scared off by his professors. The other drifted away from his faith altogether due to questions encountered during his studies. Their education did as much harm as it did good. Formal training came at a high cost, both financially and in terms of ministry left undone. As a result, at Hope Chapel we have determined to send people to seminary only *after* we have them up and running as church planters. We still school them, but only after we mentor them into a church plant.

Christian author Lyle Schaller supports this reasoning. He writes, "those who today complain that too much education can ruin a person for the pastoral ministry are echoing a five-hundred-year-old cry."[1] He goes on to note that specialization and increased education have not produced a measurably better product in medicine, law, education or religion.[2]

Locally trained clergy comprise the first part of a formula for rapid multiplication of the church.

Rent Your Meeting Space

For three decades, Hope Chapel has been launching new congregations in rented properties ranging from school gymnasiums and cafeterias to bowling alleys. This practice is not confined to Hope Chapel or to the United States. On a recent trip to Mongolia, I preached to a congregation that meets in a community center. What makes this location unique is that two other congregations meet on the premises at the same time. For many years two evangelical churches in Palo Alto, California, met under similar conditions, and both saw rapid growth. I know of a church that began in a labor union hall. Another met in a bar. One man runs small-group fellowships in Japanese karaoke parlors. Many cell churches meet in homes in third-world countries.

One man at Hope Chapel began a church-planting movement by funding a young Pakistani evangelist and teaching him to turn his converts into church planters. From the energies of these two men, 36 house churches evolved in 16 months. Their second-year goal is 100 congregations.

Rented or borrowed meeting space is the second part of the rapid multiplication equation.

You Can Move into Bivocational Ministry

The final nut has been tougher to crack. In pastoral circles there is a stigma attached to a pastor who does not receive a full-time salary from a local church. Well-meaning leaders have actually discouraged young men from continuing in pastoral ministry by stating that a bivocational leader is not a *real* pastor.

These people even criticize others who have been trained for ministry while volunteering on the staff of a local church. Fortunately this bias is changing.

Bivocational pastorates can provide the final third of the rapid multiplication formula.

Bivocational Ministry Has a Proven Track Record

As I have already noted, Scripture endorses bivocational ministry. Moreover, we can also find it woven into the fabric of our own Judeo-Christian history. Consider Rabbi Hillel, who founded a well-known rabbinic school. He worked at felling trees.[3] Read the words of Chrysostom. In the fourth century, he described the life of the rural bishops of Antioch: "These men you may see sometimes yoking the oxen and driving the plough, and again ascending the pulpit and cultivating the souls under their care; now uprooting the thorns from the earth with a hook, and now purging out the sins of the soul by the Word."[4]

Most American Christian leaders acknowledge that bivocational concepts work well in other countries. But they too often view the option as a liability rather than an asset. When a culture persecutes Christians, churches tend to remain small and pastors are forced into secular work. It is easy to overlook the fact that persecution fosters a faster rate of new-church launches. One reason this happens is because persecuted church leaders and their congregations *do not expect* to have a fully salaried pastorate. Thus, persecution of the church lowers a barrier to rapid multiplication.

What persecution bequeaths, we can easily replicate with a relatively easy change in viewpoint. The Japanese prove the point. Japan's pastors are the most educated and highest-paid clergy in the world. However, the Japanese church shows relatively little growth.[5] Hope Chapel, on the other hand, has thrived in Japan. Our church plants have been fruitful, although most of our church planters earn money in the marketplace and pastor in their spare time.

Many congregations could not exist if its members had to pay their pastor a full-time salary. Sparsely populated rural areas tend to house smaller congregations, and that makes it difficult for them to generate a pastor's salary. Churches populated with retired people shrink as members pass on to their heavenly rewards. For them, finances are a monumental problem; many live on fixed incomes. New congregations in heavily populated urban centers often face rent issues that strain finances. In each of these situations, a person bringing their own salary to the table enables ministry that otherwise would not exist.

NEIL COLE PLANTS HOUSE CHURCHES

Neil Cole, a Southern California church planter, has managed to set aside all three obstacles to rapid church multiplication. He began with a handful of people in a private residence. Today, the churches that have mushroomed out of that original group meet in homes, storefronts and office buildings. Congregations worship at parks and beaches. They even hold church in a locker room at a state university and another in a faculty lounge at a nearby community college. Meetings are held on whatever night or day works best for the members. As a result, most do not have services during the traditional Sunday-morning time slot.

Leaders are discipled within each church. New pastors are simply mature disciples with followers, which eliminates the cost of a formal education. The discipleship format is very simple. The portal for leadership development along with Christian growth is called a Life Transformation Group.[6]

Most pastors in Neil's church plants have full-time jobs in the mainstream marketplace, although some who have a regional responsibility for a network of churches are paid a small stipend by the church and serve on a bivocational basis. The antithesis of megachurches, these groups are intentionally kept small. By listening to new believers, they have discovered that a small, relational and experiential church is more desirable than a large congregation. These smaller, simple churches also multiply faster. Neil says the only people who want to grow larger groups are those who have transferred from traditional churches.

For Neil and his network of churches, the payoff is in mushrooming evangelism and the rapid proliferation of the church. They face virtually no cost for pastoral training, facilities or ministerial salaries. This unfetters the people to become church planters.

I asked Neil how many churches had been planted in four years. He gave me three astounding answers. First, he had no idea as to the total number of congregations in the movement. Second, he said that in 2001 they did know that they had planted 52 churches—that is an average of one each week. The final answer was gripping. He said they are not just multiplying disciples, leaders and churches but *movements* as well. Each movement within the parent movement has a natural affinity group, such as Awakening Student Initiatives, which started six or eight churches in one year. The initial churches Neil started were called Awakening Chapels. But these churches are now only one of the expanding networks of congregations under the umbrella of the broader ministry he directs, which is called Church Multiplication Associates. At the time of this writing, there are nine church-planting movements within the association. Their influence has spread up and down the West Coast and also extends as far as Spain, France and North Africa.

Bivocational pastors are Christian heroes and need to be treated as such. I believe we could double the number of active Christians in the West if we aggressively embraced this concept.

YOU SHOULD MEASURE THE PERILS

Not everyone is cut out to lead a congregation while they hold down another job. The schedule grinds on families and friendships. Yet creating ministry that otherwise could not exist offers a strong motive to accept a little pain. Let's separate romance from reality by looking at the personal ups and downs of bivocational ministry.

You Will Grow Weary

Two jobs can leave a person too busy and too tired to enjoy life. Yet if a person is good at delegating tasks, he or she can usually spread the work around. A reasonable goal is to commit to and achieve the same level of involvement that you would experience as the leader of a large home fellowship or adult Sunday School class in a large church.

Do Not Forget Your Family

A bivocational leader encounters more than the pressure of weariness. There is a sensory overload that accompanies such responsibility. There are a zillion details to grasp and decisions to make. The bivocational leader will have far too many fellowship opportunities and a plethora of ministry commitments. You must learn how to accept the right ones and reject the others. Even then, you will constantly be on the run.

All of this ministry can leave families without much of a leader's time. A clear commitment to priorities will solve the problem. But it requires an iron will and careful assignment of available time. I teach pastors to mark out physically (and generously) *family time* in their calendars or electronic organizers for a year ahead. That way any successful intrusion on their family time will have to be important enough to change an already established schedule.

A pastor in Southern California tells the story of a time when one of the members of his young church, insisting that there was an emergency, repeatedly called on a day the pastor had set aside for his family. The pastor finally relented and met with the man. When they got together the church member said, "Thank you for coming. There really is no emergency. I just wanted to see if you would be there for me." *Do not let this happen to you.* Only break away from your family time for true emergencies.

Take Your Sabbath Rest

Busy Americans seldom get the rest they need. For bivocational pastors, finding time for Sabbath rest is even more difficult than for full-time pastors. But the bivocational person needs this biblically mandated break more than everyone else. From a purely physical standpoint the need is obvious. More important is the need for clear-headed strategizing and decision making. Time alone with God is a necessity. Again, mark your calendar for a year in advance. People who look over your shoulder at your calendar will respect your decision to put this time ahead of their need or their plan for your life.

In the past, I often surrendered my day off to church members who would point out the empty slots on my calendar. When I began marking the calendar ahead of time, those people who had interrupted my Sabbath actually congratulated me for taking one. Marking the calendar also transfers into making personal plans for the Sabbath. If you take my advice and do this, you will have richer down times.

Establish Credibility

Another visible downside to bivocational ministry is other people's tendency to question your legitimacy. When this happens to you, take your accusers to the Scriptures and cite historical and contemporary examples of success. This will justify your cause. This is a common problem for bivocational pastors. Tom McDonald, Neil Cole and Jack Hayford all overcame it. In fact, Hayford held another job when he took over leadership of a small existing core group and "planted" The Church On The Way in Van Nuys, California. Jack even hired several staff members before he left his outside job.

One way to deal with issues that affect your credibility as a bivocational pastor is to discuss them openly with your core-team members and to bring them into your weekend teaching as real-life illustrations of your ministry. Discuss both the negative aspects I have noted and the benefits listed in the section below.

Let your people know why you chose the bivocational route. Help them understand what it costs you personally. Teach them what they gain as a congregation from not paying you a full-time salary.

Teach the metaphors of Scripture that define the church as the "Body of Christ," "a city" and other unifying images. Build an appreciation for teamwork around the sacrifices you and your family make for the church. Help each person realize his or her own role in the family. Train your people toward the concept of full ministry potential in every person. Make your bivocational situation something to be proud of rather than just a difficulty with which you live.

Finally, if you plan bivocational ministry as a step toward a full-time situation, make your church members and supporters aware of your timetable. Keeping everyone informed is the foundation of credibility.

BE SURE TO COUNT THE BENEFITS

On the positive side of the ledger, the bivocational pastor enjoys some strong benefits.

Mingle with the Crowd

One benefit is face-to-face communication with the people in the community you are trying to evangelize.

Let's start here by looking at the frustrations of a full-time church planter. I planted the first Hope Chapel as a faith mission. I told God that I would pastor as long as He could supply my financial needs. I informed Him that if I ever had to take a job, I would quit the pastorate. The church grew, and He supplied the cost of living in an expensive Southern California beach town. But the answer to my prayers generated growth-restricting problems.

First, I did not know what to do with 40 hours of ministry time each week while shepherding fewer than 100 people. I was bored, lonely and often frustrated. I would devote whole days to prayer and Bible reading only to fall asleep on the office floor. I would awake to feelings of despair and disappointment.

The second problem was my inability to set the tone for personal evangelism. New to the community, I had few non-Christian friends. A secular job would have allowed me to evangelize coworkers. It would have established my example as a role model for evangelism in the church.

Finally, I was frustrated by the "let the pastor do it—it's what we pay him for" syndrome. It would have been much easier for me to teach the concept of Body ministry (see Eph. 4:15-16) if I had a job like everybody else.

Enjoy Your Career

Another vote for bivocational pastorates is the ability to keep up a career (at least until the church demands full-time attention). I know lawyers, doctors, contractors and others who chose the bivocational route into ministry simply because they enjoy their business life and do not want to lose it. Dan Lucero planted a church in France as a student while there on a Fulbright scholarship. He continued to pastor after receiving his degree. Between weekends he now travels the world as an environmental research expert. His church thrives as one of the fastest-growing evangelical congregations in that country. People like Dan remain bivocational as a preference.

The Extra Capital Helps

Bivocational pastors bring extra financial capital to the new church. This is the most obvious benefit. Churches can be planted that could not otherwise exist. A bivocational approach spares a congregation many thousands of dollars per year in operating capital. This is a way of taking the gospel into the byways as well as the highways and urging people into Christ's kingdom (see Luke 14:23, *KJV*).

You Can Bless Your Family

A bivocational lifestyle can put extra money into a pastor's pocket. Rather than live on a scrimpy budget, a bivocational pastor in a small community can supply those things he longs for his family to enjoy.

Small churches do not always pay well when they do provide a full-time salary. If we make full-time ministry into the holy grail, pastors are unable to do all they should do for their families, such as send their kids to college. While God will always meet our basic needs, a parent wants the best things for his children—sometimes he even wants to buy them Nikes. A bivocational pastor who is a good steward and moves in wisdom can provide some of these things for his family, whereas some single-salary situations condemn a family to near poverty.

You will face enough problems and angst along the way as you plant a church. Feeling guilty about your family not having its needs met does not need to be one of them. Bivocational ministry solves this dilemma.

Be a One-Person Support Agency
One final benefit to this approach is that it provides the ability of an individual to start a church if denominational or parent-church financial support is minimal or not available. But once again note: You always need to be sent out by a parent church.

THE DECISION IS ULTIMATELY YOURS

Bivocational ministry is not easy. But it does open doors that would otherwise remain shut. The decision to pay this price should be carefully weighed against family needs and the sense of calling in your life. I would only recommend this road to people who possess strong familial support and only in situations that actually dictate it. Urban or rural church plants may require a bivocational approach. Limited parent-church or denominational funding many also force this to be an option.

The one place I do not believe that bivocational ministry is effective is when it is used as a mask for a lack of results. If a pastor has to take a job because the ministry is not working out, it may be a sign that he has missed God's direction or that God is trying to head the pastor out of the situation.

In the end, only you can decide the viability of bivocational service as you weigh it against your calling, the needs of your family and the dictates of your chosen community.

CHURCH PLANTER'S CHECKLIST

1. List all of the reasons why a bivocational role would be good in your situation.
2. List the ways that bivocational ministry would impede progress toward your goals.

3. Write a rationale for either a full-time salary or a bivocational setup. Fill at least two pages.

4. Include the results of question three in your budget.

Notes

1. Lyle E. Schaller, *It's a Different World* (Nashville, TN: Abingdon Press, 1987), p. 198.

2. Ibid., pp. 200-211.

3. Neil Braun, *Laity Mobilized: Reflections on Church Growth in Japan and Other Lands* (Grand Rapids, MI: William B. Eerdmans, 1971), p. 38.

4. W. Ream, "The Support of the Clergy in the First Five Centuries A.D.," *International Review of Missions* (October 1956), p. 424.

5. Otis Carey, *Protestant Missions*, Vol. 2, *A History of Christianity in Japan* (Tokyo: Charles E. Tuttle Company, 1976), pp. 163, 296.

6. Neil Cole and Bob Logan, *Cultivating a Life for God: Multiplying Disciples Through Life Transformation Groups* (Carol Stream, IL: ChurchSmart Resources, 1999), n.p.

CHAPTER 10

BUILDINGS:
WHERE *SHOULD* YOU MEET?

The first Christians met in homes and in public spaces. Today, as the Church rapidly multiplies itself, believers still congregate in nontraditional places. Some groups begin in homes, others in larger structures. But leaders in every church, if they want to see their congregation grow, must understand real estate and its effects on congregational life.

We started the first Hope Chapel in an empty church building. It was designed to hold 66 people. We stretched the space to fit more than 200 by moving walls. We seated people on the floor, in the aisles and outside, where they had to look through the windows to see the service. We also added services in a nearby community center, conducted children's ministries at a nearby pre-school, utilized a converted garage and found a way to operate in a large steel shed. Later we obtained a long-vacant bowling alley that became our permanent headquarters. The bowling alley enabled our attendance to mushroom into the thousands.

By contrast, we started Hope Chapel Kaneohe Bay on the beach in Kailua. Over the years, we operated in several locations—including a community center, two public schools and three office buildings—before we obtained a permanent worship location.

Both original spots had their benefits as well as distractions. The church building in California was available 24 hours a day, seven days a week and offered great storage. Furthermore, we owned it, so we paid no rent. But it had only seven parking spaces—a limitation that created massive problems. The beach in Hawaii was exquisite (once voted most beautiful in the world), had great parking and featured tremendous amenities. The biggest problem was that we had no permit. There was a policeman who looked askance at us each week as he drove through the parking lot two-thirds of the way through my message. However, if I had to choose one place I have started a church over all others, I would opt for the beach. The sandy, windblown sanctuary gets my vote because it was temporary. We easily abandoned it for better quarters, moving five times before we bought a more permanent location. The church building in California limited our thinking, hence our growth. We remained chained to it for five years.

Flexible thinking and multiple locations will free you to grow at God's pace. Tying yourself down to one spot only creates a growth-restricting obstacle. After the experience on the beach in Hawaii, I became aware of the need for church leaders to keep their minds open regarding meeting facilities.

At Hope Chapel, as a way of freeing our concerns from building-related restrictions, we devised a very large church campus. In a notebook we placed photographs and descriptions of all the locations available to us for ancillary church meetings, whether we owned them, had to rent them or could use them free of charge. Our extended campus included three community centers, a Catholic seminary, various hotels and camps, four public schools and many great homes—if we had owned it all it would have been worth more than a quarter of a billion dollars. We rejoiced that our heavenly Father made so many of His resources available to us at such a low cost and virtually on demand. But we would not have had so many possibilities if we had restricted our activities to a traditional church campus.

My point is that buildings shape *your* thinking. Most often they restrict rather than liberate you. Try to broaden your perspective as we look at potential meeting sites for your new congregation.

THERE ARE UPSIDES TO TEMPORARY SPACE

The church I pastor has relocated to "permanent quarters." However, for us it is just our *current* location. Although we believe our new campus is a gift from God, we are already trying to expand our activities onto an adjacent college campus. To do less would build a box around the future growth and flexibility of our church.

There are several reasons why every church—especially a new plant—should prefer temporary facilities.

It Allows Flexibility

Viewing a church campus as permanent is very restrictive. Nothing is permanent except God Himself. Your campus is not really permanent because you will eventually outgrow it, or your people may move to another neighborhood and you may decide to follow them. If you view your location as permanent, the blessing it provides could turn into a curse. If you see your facility as your *current temporary location*, you maintain the mental ability to grow beyond its boundaries or move where the harvest is ripest.

It Eliminates Major Capital Outlay

If you opt for a series of temporary locations, you will not face high rental payments until you have a larger congregation and can afford to pay them.

Some denominations mortgage a piece of property at the outset of a church plant. Although those groups have good intentions, they often unwittingly saddle young churches with expensive real estate. As a result, they unintentionally leverage the church plant against growth.

I advise church planters to grow a congregation without owning land or buildings for at least five years. Try to rent space for a *few hours per week* rather than leasing property that you will pay for 24 hours per day, seven days a week. Obtain space to hold twice as many people as you expect in the next three months. Hold multiple services so you get full use of your rent money. We hold five celebration services in our church each weekend and may have expanded to six by the time this book is published. I would not dream of starting a church without at least two meetings on Sunday morning, because it would be poor stewardship of real estate.

The goal here is to use the church's funds efficiently. Renting space is an operational cost, which you want to limit. As I noted before, you should spend a greater amount of money on outreach.

It Reduces Distractions

Too many church planters get hung up on the goal of finding the *ultimate* building. When you put off the purchase of property for five years, you do not have to handle major real-estate distractions at a time when you need to be building people. A property acquisition, construction or remodeling program always shifts the pastor and core group's focus away from evangelism and discipleship.

If you delay the acquisition of property, you will not be distracted by real estate details, but you will still think about growth and your eventual physical needs. Ironically, you probably will discover a wonderful location, but at a horrible time. The building I found just a few weeks after planting Hope Chapel in California eventually became ours. Fortunately, however, we did not attempt to buy the place for more than three years. We did pray all along and we occupied it in our fifth year. Had we spent those first three years pursuing that facility, we would have lost momentum.

Helpful Hint: When you find your "perfect" building, put it out of your mind and concentrate on the work at hand. This advice applies to the purchase of your personal residence as well. Rent for the first year or two. Do not allow yourself to get hung up on a remodeling project or new home purchase while you are planting a church. If you do that you will never have enough time for ministry, let alone your family.

It Keeps Expectations in Check

A series of rented facilities keeps members much happier than a semi-permanent location. This is because short-term facilities *feel* temporary. This is similar to the feeling you get on a camping trip. When pitching a tent in the great outdoors, you do not expect a nicely-tiled bathroom or plush carpet. Instead you accept basic services with a sense of thanksgiving. Campers seldom engage in turf wars within their own campsites. They know that whatever boundaries they might tack down will change sooner rather than later.

Church members come with expectations, especially the ones who have been involved in another church. They can place enormous demands on leadership. Temporary facilities temper these expectations. Maintain the camping aura and your people will be less demanding of the service aspects of ministry and more willing to contribute time and energy to providing those services. They will appreciate little niceties rather than complain about the color of the walls. They will be less concerned over ownership of space and more willing to share tools and resources. The time you spend in rented quarters will eventually glow in your memory as the "good old days when we all really pulled together." Do not fight the good times while you live in them.

It Provides Easy Entry into Ministry
When you operate a portable church in a temporary facility, you need a huge workforce. This is a blessing. One of the downsides of my church's move to our own campus is the loss of available jobs that easily engage and involve newcomers. When we met in public schools we enjoyed recruiting new, sometimes non-Christian people to the task of setting up and tearing down our operation each week. As simple an act as folding chairs at the end of the service brought first-timers into action. We would recruit for other tasks among those who helped without asking. Most of those we invited to serve were pleased that they had been invited onto the team. Virtually all of our current pastoral team members say they first got involved in ministry by helping stack chairs at the end of a service.

YOU CAN OPERATE A RENT-FREE OFFICE

When you launch your church you will be looking for ways to keep costs down. With this in mind, it is appropriate and useful to ask questions that most new pastors would never have asked in past years. Do you need a centralized location? Are there ways you can organize, communicate, operate and lead your church without the traditional pastor office?

"The office" means different things to different people, but if you are creative you can meet your needs in other, low-cost ways.

An Office Full of Frills Often Kills

Office space can become a status symbol in any field. I once heard a stock analyst being interviewed on television. He suggested that the amount of money spent on office space is a predictor of success or failure in a start-up business. He said that the fancier the office, the more likely the failure. Lean operations do not include marble floors and carpeted walls. Many of the failed dotcoms of the 1990s underscored the stock analyst's observation. Amazon.com, on the other hand, started in a garage using unframed doors as desktops. Hewlett-Packard also started in a garage. The same principle applies to a church plant.

A Virtual Office Keeps You Connected

Pastors, paid staff members and volunteer staff can better stay in touch if you create a virtual office.

Cell phones and e-mail are great communication tools. An unadvertised website with simple passwords for entry can provide centralized files for all but sensitive financial information. A coffee shop is a great place to do counseling. Large homes provide wonderful meeting spaces. You can collect mail through a commercial post-office box.

An office provides four basic functions: communications, storage, meeting space and a mailbox. Find a way to supply each function at no cost, and you have created a virtual office.

A Headquarters Gives You a Place to Gather

There is a fifth function an office provides, although it is not crucial at the beginning of your church life. I call it the "clubhouse effect." Your people will eventually want a place that they can view as headquarters for your operation. The primary need served is the ability for them to drop by and see someone they know. At this point, the office begins to give a sense of permanence to a new congregation. Try to delay that fifth function as long as possible.

Helpful Hint: A well-developed and interactive website can function as a clubhouse for a while. Spend your money on technology rather than rent for as long as you can. The best technology is still cheaper than monthly payments to a landlord. It is also more flexible.

Someone Else's Office Has a Desk You Can Fill

When you grow—which every successful church plant should do—you will eventually need rented office space. One pastor I know saves money by subletting space in an office belonging to a member of the church which launched him. He spends $200 per month for a really nice setup. He has no secretary, but he enjoys the support of the owner's receptionist who collects his mail and answers basic questions about his whereabouts. He is also able to take advantage of the supply network surrounding the owner's business. The people he rents from already know the best places to buy goods and services. Finally, he has evangelized several of the people working in that office and thus has been growing his church.

There are many businesses with unused office space. Often the owners will welcome a few extra dollars each month. If I were planting a church, I would start with realtors. Real-estate offices *often* contain a few empty desks. This is because the real-estate market fluctuates in fairly regular cycles. Brokers cannot afford to move between large and small quarters at every whim of the market. Real-estate offices are also designed around the needs of on-site interaction with clients. This translates into nice reception areas and small conference rooms.

Until you are forced into a relationship with a traditional landlord, look for every way to reduce or eliminate real estate costs. For most churches this is the second-highest expense after salaries.

LOCATION IS EVERYTHING

The three most important words you can memorize when renting meeting space are "location, location and location." Location is everything to the prospective church member. The place must help meet his or her needs. A church's location should be accessible, adequate in size, equipped with surplus parking and have a pleasant ambience.

Look for an Accessible Site

A pastor I know once told me that people will drive 50 miles to church, but they will not pass through more than 12 stoplights. I am not sure how scientific of an observation he made. However, I do know that most large churches are located near freeways. I also know that the big downtown churches of the last century lost many members even after they added adequate parking. They were too far from the suburbs. You must locate your church where it is easy to find and easy to access.

Consider the Size of Your Space

I once talked with a man in a rural community who wanted to move a congregation from a living room to an oversized double garage. He assured me that the church would remodel the garage to make it feel as pleasant as the living room. His vision was simply too small.

First, it is always easy to add 100 percent more space to your facility by simply adding a second (or third) weekend service. I can still remember driving home from a meeting with Dr. Gene A. Getz when he described the early growth of the Fellowship Bible Churches in Texas. They held services on Friday evenings, Sunday mornings, Sunday afternoons and Sunday evenings. Each meeting was two hours long, and they held a coffee break between the worship and the teaching. As I drove I rejoiced that Getz had given me a $2-million idea—that was the value of our building at that time. We could gain another full use of our facility simply by adding a Friday service to our schedule.

Eventually you have to move beyond adding meetings. You will truly *need* larger facilities. When you do, think as big as you can. Twice the size of your short-term needs should be a minimum if you have to sign a long-term lease. If you are renting public facilities on a short lease or month-to-month basis, you do not have to be so expansive—you can always move again as your needs overtake you.

As you grow, someone will introduce you to either the two-thirds or the 80-percent rule. These rules-of-thumb call for you to never consistently fill a meeting space to over two-thirds or 80 percent of its capacity—depending upon who states the rule. I stay away from these formulas because while I think they are true over the long term, I have seen them beautifully violated by the Holy Spirit during times of revival. Sometimes crammed space actually contributes to growth. I do not introduce these percentages to my church because I do not want to limit God.

Secure More Parking Than You Need

I constantly sneak out and prowl our parking lots during worship services. I want to be sure that people find it *easy* to locate a parking spot. The emphasis here is on *ease* of parking. Our people come at a rate of 2.3 persons per car. This is partly because of the number of married couples and families in our congregation. When there were more single people in our church, there were 1.9 people per car. We know how many our auditorium and children's areas can accommodate. Simple math tells us how many parking spaces it takes to fill the meeting space to capacity. We also know that it takes about 15 percent *surplus* parking to allow us to consistently fill our interior spaces. Our people simply will not hunt that hard for a place. Therefore, we try to provide enough empty spaces so that parking is easy to find.

Your members will always discover places to park their cars. First-time guests will not. You have to make it easy for them. Hence, you should be sure a prospective location provides plenty of parking. If it does not, look elsewhere.

Find a Building with Soul
Buildings need soul. This is that elusive quality that makes a building special. Soul may reside in a quirky history. It may include a great view. Perhaps the building has great architecture. Maybe your building is so ugly that you can capitalize on its appearance. Church on the beach has obvious soul. So does our current facility with an ocean view so expansive that you think you can see all the way to Tahiti. When choosing between two locations, opt for the one that gets people talking.

Here Are Some Ideas for Locations
The earliest Christians met in many different places for worship and fellowship. We know they gathered in the Temple in Jerusalem and in homes (see Acts 2:41-47). In Philippi they worshiped in a place of prayer near a river (see Acts 16:13-16). At Berea they met in a synagogue (see Acts 17:10-11). Paul preached in the marketplace. Jesus held meetings on the seashore (see

Matt. 13:1-2) and on a mountaintop (see Matt. 5:1-2). We should find license in their actions to get out of our mental boxes and into whatever space is available.

Robert Schuller started the Crystal Cathedral in a drive-in theater. Mike MacIntosh of Harvest Christian Fellowship in San Diego used an old fixed-screen theater. John Osteen launched Lakewood Church in a Houston, Texas, feed store. Some have used restaurants, storefronts and nightclubs. In Hawaii we have a church in just about every public school. In Latin America, preachers hold meetings in great stadiums.

One Hope Chapel started an outreach church on a vacant lot in the skid-row of a large American city. A friend in Okinawa moved a baby church to a hotel ballroom. Daniel Brown's Coastlands Church in Aptos, California, started in an old estate house, moved to a community college lecture hall and now meets in what once was a convent.

Grace Church in Nashua, New Hampshire, bought a half-million-square-foot factory that once made blankets for the Union Army during the Civil War. Jim Reeve's Faith Community Church in West Covina, California, purchased the plant where the Stealth bomber was developed. I once held a large Sunday-morning Bible study in a town hall provided rent free by a local bank as a community center.

Hope Chapel in Hermosa Beach bought a bowling alley and a supermarket. Hope Chapel in Kihei, Maui, turned a warehouse into a beautiful church facility. New Hope Church on Oahu uses a high school with a video-feed into a beautifully remodeled overflow space in a nearby industrial complex. My Japanese friends recently discovered an oversupply of karaoke rooms quite rentable for church planting and small-group meetings.

We control the initial decision as to where we will meet. But from that point on, our location controls us. Be sure you are controlled in a manner that ensures rather than hinders growth.

CHURCH PLANTER'S CHECKLIST

1. Describe the functions you would assign to rented office space.
2. What technology would you need to serve a core staff of seven people without renting office space?
3. List 10 possible temporary office locations to ready yourself for the day when you need larger, more traditional office space.
4. List 15 potential meeting locations for a new church in the city or town where you intend to plant. Prioritize the list according to the planned growth of the new church.
5. Write out the pros and cons attached to the top seven locations on your list.
6. Begin to research the possibility of renting the facilities you have listed.

CHAPTER 11

NECESSARY RELATIONSHIPS:
HOW TO PLAN
WHAT YOU MAY NOT
UNDERSTAND

In Hawaii we rented our first public school for services six months into the life of our church. I was still a newcomer. This meant that I dressed and spoke like a tourist who thought he was a local. In other words, a lot about my demeanor was somewhat offensive or at least contemptuous to people who grew up in the community.

The relationship with the school leadership was rocky. I did not seem to communicate with the principal. I made many mistakes, and they always magnified into crises. One day I took my secretary along to a meeting with the principal. While waiting to see him, she struck up a conversation with his secretary. This woman had previously been very cold toward me. My secretary found an opportunity to explain the church and its mission. She explained why she trusted me and my plans for our church. She even made jokes, apologizing for my funny clothes and odd speech. When the principal came to greet us, his secretary went out of her way to introduce me to him with great respect. Actually, she tipped him off that she had now accepted me into her world. During our meeting, my secretary casually gave him the same rundown that she had given his secretary. He and I became friends that day. Our problems immediately diminished. And the principal eventually accepted the Lord through the efforts of one of our members who was on his faculty.

New relationships always carry the burden of potential misunderstanding. For the church planter, this means that he will face a host of communication problems. Most of those covered in this chapter may seem insignificant at a time when you want to focus on evangelism and growth strategies, but they are necessary to your success. To the degree that you cultivate these six relationships, you will prevent communication breakdowns and walk along a smooth path to spiritual victory.

GET ALONG WITH YOUR LANDLORD

Your landlord can hurt you in ways that no one else can. Will you get bumped from the community center some weekend for another neighborhood activity? Will the principal defend you if someone challenges your right to meet in a public school? Do you have to hire a janitor to open and close the property? Will the landlord trust you with keys to the facility?

This relationship is crucial and can be unforgiving. Yet it is not too hard to get right. Clear communication goes a long way toward establishing and maintaining a solid relationship. A humble and serving heart helps, too.

Designate a Communicator

Just before moving to Hawaii, I met a pastor who had held church services in a large mortuary chapel for 11 years. He gave me this wonderful advice: "Appoint one person to communicate with the people you rent from. Ask the landlord to do likewise. Allow no exchanges other than through those two people."

Many churches get into trouble because they never learn the value of a designated communicator. When three or four people on one side speak to two or three on the other, conflict and confusion is likely to emerge. A single channel of communication insures that there is only one version of any plan or calendar. Appoint someone you trust. If possible, this should be a person who has a preexisting relationship with your landlord. Keep in close contact with this person, but stay out of his or her way. You will have fewer troubles.

Have a Humble Heart

You should view your rental contract as an act of God's grace. Thank Him for it. Also, thank the people who control the property for their kindness toward you. If you rent a public building, your rent money will probably go to a central office, the parks department or the board of education. The people who actually put up with you will incur extra expense and may *not* be reimbursed for it. Therefore, do not act like you are entitled to the property or any correlating services. Keep a thankful heart, and you will maintain a humble spirit. Develop an arrogant and demanding attitude, and you are on the way out of favor—and most likely out of a meeting place.

Go the Extra Mile

Jesus said we should volunteer to walk an extra mile when asked to carry someone's load. His advice certainly applies to the church in rented quarters. You can win your landlord's heart by going the extra distance. See the rent as the first mile. Beautification projects and favors are the second.

At Hope Chapel, we have found ways to help beautify the office buildings that we lease. At one such facility the neighborhood kids repeatedly trampled the landscape and broke a fence when they used the property as a shortcut. We asked permission to repair the fence and planted colorful thorn bushes to discourage trespassers. Once we replaced damaged hall carpet when we redecorated our own space. Flowers in an outside planter box brought a smile to the landlord's face.

In Hawaii we operated for 14 years in one public school. We paid low rent to the school district. This low overhead allowed us to raise an average of $15,000 per year for projects that ranged from cancer treatment for a student to campus beautification. We assembled a team to clean graffiti. We partnered with the school and the local police to warn parents about the latest drugs available to their kids. We teamed up with the school to sponsor a debate between gubernatorial candidates. We held workdays to clean up the campus before the first day of school, painted two classrooms and painted the cafeteria each year.

The people who work at the school like us, and we like them. During our last two years there we were repeatedly told that the administration had decided that we were a permanent part of the school family and that our leaving was "forbidden." Many years have passed since we finally left for other quarters, but we maintain an ongoing relationship with the principal, the vice principal and faculty. We have also been able to continue tutoring students on the campus. Our friendship has allowed us to intervene in a positive manner in situations where other churches had been in conflict with the school district. For us, the relationship with the school and the school district became a wonderful bridge into the community. Many people have become members of our church as a result.

Make New Friends

Build a relationship with the landlord's assistants, and you will have the friendship of their employer. Offend them, and you are in big trouble. Go out of your way to brighten the lives of these very important people—janitors, secretaries, accountants and others.

A bouquet of flowers or a dozen chocolate chip cookies can make a secretary smile whenever she thinks of your church. Janitors love cookies, too. A small box of candy dropped off to the assistants every time you go in to meet your landlord will accomplish the same results. Most churches display flowers on Sundays. Why not pass them on when Monday morning rolls around? What about all those poinsettias at Christmas or lilies at Easter? If left at the front desk of a public school, they can brighten the day of a bunch of teachers who have to share their classrooms with your Sunday School.

SET UP PROPER FINANCIAL SYSTEMS

The apostle Paul taught us to live in submission to the government (see Rom. 13:1-5). His advice should extend to financial institutions. There is not a lot of necessary advice here except "just do it." You need to be covered by a 501c3 nonprofit corporation, legal banking services and proper accounting.

The corporation may be your denomination or, if you are independent, you may need to organize one. Less than a thousand dollars and the help of a local attorney will get you set up. This step is vital, because your bank will not allow you to open a business account without an employer identification number, which comes with creation of the corporation. Taxes must be paid, including quarterly self-employment taxes for pastors and withholding taxes for nonpastoral employees. You will also need to develop a system of internal financial records, including an annual budget, a disbursement system and donation records.

> **Helpful hint:** It should go without noting that churches should not operate in an underground economy. Do not be tempted to see this as a way to cut corners. It is actually a way to go to jail and to sully the gospel.

You should subscribe to a few legal and tax newsletters available to churches and other nonprofit entities. They often have more up-to-date advice than banks or attorneys. This is because they specialize in church and nonprofit finances.

I noted earlier in this book the importance of your relationships with your parent church and denominational leaders. As you establish new, exciting friendships and connections in the community where you are planting your church, do not forget those who have helped get you there.

Maintain a Parent-Church Relationship

Your parents define you during the early years of your life. The same is true for your spiritual parents. The church that sponsors you hands off more than money and a baton of leadership. It provides credibility and a spiritual heritage. Pastors we launch succeed if they pay attention to this relationship. Those that ignore it or attempt to break away always falter. They soon lose focus, becoming the product of the latest seminar they attended rather than the value system we attempted to teach them.

Members of the Corinthian church divided their loyalties among four different groups. Paul, their founder, rebuked their foolishness. He pointed them to Jesus as the Lord over their activities. But he also unashamedly called himself their spiritual father. He asked for their continued friendship. He also asked that they prioritize his wisdom over that of their other teachers. He identified anything short of this as arrogance on their parts (see 1 Cor. 4:14-19).

You do not have to imitate your mentors in every action. You do need their continued input and the spiritual heritage they bring to your young church. Both times I have personally planted churches, the credibility I had came from those who sent me long before it rested on my own deeds.

Your relationship with your parents impacts your own ability to raise children. This is also true in church. If the church you plant relates well to those who sent you, you will easily multiply your ministry throughout the earth. Break from your spiritual parents and you can be sure of a dysfunctional relationship with leaders you train. Whatever you sow, you really will reap.

Embrace Your Denomination

I have never been a flag waver, yet I am loyal to my denomination. To me, a denomination is less a spiritual entity and more a matter of pragmatism. It presents me with a great opportunity to pool resources and develop lasting friendships. My attitudes vastly affect my relationship with it.

If I saw my denomination as a spiritual entity, I would hesitate to question its policies because I would see them as directives from God. At the same time, I would feel obligated to leave the denomination if I found it flawed in any way. Seeing the movement as a human institution gives me freedom to disagree with it. My view also allows me to remain loyal even though I may not agree with every current policy. I would never think of abandoning my own family because they lack perfection. Why would I leave my denominational family over their mistakes and misgivings? The Scriptures adjure us to submit to human institutions as ministers of God. If this applies to secular government, it must also speak of church denominations (see Rom. 13:1-7).

Working with a denomination can be tricky. There are certain obvious obligations. These usually involve a tithe or some sort of financial commitment. They extend to missions giving, generation of reports and attendance at conferences or conventions. What may not be spelled out is the expected use of denominationally published materials and curricula, participation in camps and rallies, etc.

Many of these unspecified obligations fall under the category of cooperation. That word is a red flag to me. When I hear someone ask me to cooperate, I ask them exactly what they mean. I want to know if I am required to participate or if I am free to meet the needs of my people in the best and most creative way I know. Usually the act of asking the question generates the freedom I crave. Denominations do a great job when providing materials and programs for smaller churches that have existed for more than a decade. However, these same tools may restrict a larger church or a new congregation on the cutting edge of evangelism. The key here is to learn to negotiate the minefield of other people's expectations. Remember, hidden expectations can injure good friendships.

Partner with People at a Local Level

When we started our church in Hawaii, we were nearly coerced into joining a nearby fellowship of pastors. The leader had established himself as the spiritual king over the community. He demanded respect and participation. When we resisted, he got ugly. We never joined, and not long after that he returned to the mainland, leaving the group without a successor. This stood in sharp contrast to the two pastoral circles I joined in California. One was a prayer-and-share meeting with some very humble men. The other had a community-service bent, and we seldom prayed. In both cases we enjoyed a solidarity rooted in our need for fellowship and partnership in the faith. The moral of this illustration is "Be selective where you invest your time."

There will always be more invitations than you can handle. You will soon be invited to join the chamber of commerce, several service clubs and one or more circles of pastors. You will also be inundated with requests for money or for congregational participation in various efforts to educate or evangelize your community. Do not say yes to all of them or you will not have any time left to plant your church.

Whenever you are tempted by these invitations, you need to fall back on your statement of purpose and your mission statement. Only involve yourself or your congregation in projects or organizations that actually serve or advance your *stated* mission. Be polite, but back away from all others. The same advice goes for traveling teachers or evangelists who want a shot at your pulpit. God called you into the community with a specific mission. Anything that does not support it detracts from it. Be involved, but build boundaries.

While hypercooperation will nullify growth, you may find opportunities to build some rather creative alliances. Long after we stopped renting from the school system, we continue to tutor children in public schools. We also join with the schools and police in an antidrug alliance we initiated. We work with our local mall and various businesses to develop pride in our community. One result is that the mall allows us to use their parking lots for large-scale community-service or evangelism events.

Our strong bent toward community service won the favor of the mayor and city fathers of Honolulu. Their friendship helped us through a major construction project and rolled over into favor with the newspapers. The key here is to prioritize your time and energy. Do not waste it. Invest it wisely in alliances that further the gospel in your community. If you build your use of time around your spiritual priorities, you will find your church operating as a "light of the world—like a city on a mountain, glowing in the night for all to see" (Matt. 5:14).

Impanel a Personal Prayer Team

Are you capable of fulfilling your dreams without God's assistance, or do you need supernatural help? If you have them covered, they are probably of your own invention. If they seem fairly impossible, they probably came from heaven. If God authored your dreams, you will *need* prayer support. You should put together a network of people who will pray for you on a regular basis.

A prayer team is *different* from a financial support network. Many of us are accustomed to calling a fund-raising piece a prayer letter. But there is a difference between the two. You should have some sort of monthly device soliciting prayer and financial support for a new ministry. However, you also need to communicate with a team of intercessors much more often. I have a team of people spread over the world who pray for me. They get a weekly e-mail message called simply Pray for Ralph. In times of crisis I contact them more often. I started the group by soliciting people from our congregation and personal friends. Later, someone suggested I allow friends to volunteer for the prayer team through our website. I was surprised to find many of my old friends wanted to join the prayer team, even though they had long since moved away from our community.

The prayer team members are faithful intercessors. Some go beyond prayer and extend their ministry functions as eyes, ears, arms and legs. They glean information pertaining to prayer problems. They volunteer their time as God calls them to climb a level higher in their prayer life in specific circumstances. These people are an essential part of my church and its success around the globe. A similar team will be imperative to the success of your church plant.

CHURCH PLANTER'S CHECKLIST

1. List the 10 most important people on the horizon of your new church.
2. Identify five things your congregation could do to win favor with your landlord.
3. Identify six spiritual needs in your chosen community that you could address even while your church is very young and relatively underdeveloped.
4. Describe a format for soliciting prayer that you will use apart from any fund-raising efforts.
5. Now act on your answers. Start to correspond with the people you have listed in this chapter.

CHAPTER 12

KICKOFF:
STEPS YOU CAN TAKE TOWARD GATHERING A CROWD

I remember a great story about the birth of Crossroads Community Church in a small town in the Pacific Northwest. For two weeks, a series of advertisements appeared in the local newspaper announcing "Crossroads is Coming!" The second round of ads sported a logo, but no explanation of what the word "Crossroads" meant or why it was coming. After four weeks the announcements added a date but still maintained the mystery. By that time the town was abuzz with speculation over what Crossroads might be. Some thought it was the name of a new movie. Others surmised that it was a new restaurant. The final ad disclosed the surprise answer and revealed that Crossroads was a great new church meeting in the local high school.

When people arrived, they found a church unlike any other. After a session of lively music and a sermon in which the pastor described the goals of the church, the visitors were asked, "Do you want this church to continue?" When the applause died down, the people were told they were participants in an election. They could vote for the future of the church at a dollar per vote. They could do this by placing their offerings in a large trash can just inside the exit. Everyone could cast as many ballots as they chose. Nearly 1 percent of that small community showed up the first week. Attendance climbed steadily in the following weeks. Income was never a problem.

The leaders of that infant church had held the people of that small town in suspense for nearly a month. After opening day, they owned the gossip wires among the residents. Their ads bred anticipation. Their methods fed speculation—even dissension. This innovative church plant absolutely captivated the attention and imagination of the community.

In one way or another, you need to do the same thing. Let's look at five factors that affect the kickoff of a new congregation.

BUILD IN GREATNESS

Will your congregation encounter greatness on opening day? People are tired of the status quo. Americans love new and innovative ideas. They also love big plays in sports, in business—even in church. This is why you need to plan something great for God.

What is your vision? If it fails to address needs, no one will pay attention. If it addresses real human problems, people will listen. Is it large enough? If it is a slam dunk, it is probably too small to attract much attention. If it is bigger than you and your abilities, it will catch fire in the hearts of those who hear it.

Picture this: 72 people gathered for our first weekend meeting in Oahu. We met, illegally, on a beach under a tree. We looked pretty fly-by-night to any casual observer. Our bulletin and our vision were the only things that *positively* differentiated us from the other churches in the community. That bulletin cost a lot of money and was probably the most expensive in any church on the island that Sunday. Our vision was definitely bigger than the others. We announced that we were planting more than one congregation that day. Our goal was to plant enough churches to include 1 percent of the population of Hawaii in just 10 years. At that time, only 4 percent of the people in the state identified themselves as Christians. At just 10,000 people, our goal was large but reachable. We presented it as 100 congregations of 100 people. Some thought it a great idea and planned to help pastor those churches. Others—a lot of them—thought we were crazy. But with one announcement we owned the imagination of both groups. We also got a lot of free publicity as they went home and filled the grapevine with our intentions.

Management guru Tom Peters describes companies and workers that educate themselves toward "towering competence."[1] For us, towering competence represented the history of church planting I brought with me from California. It gathered life in our plan to evangelize the largely Buddhist and Mormon population of Hawaii. Our finances soon reflected our people's confidence in our vision and competence. Every time we planted a new church, our per-capita income grew. Two decades later reports of church-planting activity still tend to lift our offerings. Our early goals certainly affected evangelism. People want to play on a winning team. It is easier to bring people to Christ in an environment where the goals and plans spark enthusiasm than where they do not.

Define Your Mission Field

Who do you want to reach? Do those kinds of people live in the community you have targeted? Demographics is important to the launch of a new congregation. You cannot reach people who are not living in the community. It is also difficult to evangelize people who rest comfortably in materialism with no felt need for God. You need to understand who *senses* spiritual hunger and learn how to approach them.

I wrote a book titled *Friends: The Key to Reaching Generation X.* In it I detailed the attitudes and spiritual formatting that separate this generation from all others. My research revealed that Gen-Xers are 30 percent less likely to attend church than all other adults and 44 percent less likely to be born again than Baby Boomers. They are somewhat insulated against the gospel. Yet they think highly of Christianity and are much more likely to admit to a personal spiritual search than are people of other adult generations.[2] This means that they are reachable.

Generation X is the second largest generational grouping in United States history. In the first years of the new millennium, the bulk of Gen-Xers will approach the power years when family formulation and job position converge to grant them stability, spending power and the ability to decide the future of our country. Generation X represents a great mission field with huge potential for church growth. How will you minister to these people? Unless you plant a new church in a retirement village or next to a college campus, it is likely that Gen-Xers will fill many of the seats in your services.

Each generation demands different approaches to ministry. What appeals to one will turn off another. Yet enough people like adventure and diversity that whomever you appeal to will not totally limit the scope of your new congregation. We have had older people criticize our music or ministry style and leave the church. But for every one who did, two more came because they wanted to worship with a younger congregation that was doing great things for God. The important issue for us was that we singled out one population of people as our *primary* mission. After that, we tailored everything we did to meet its needs. Ministry style grew out of our mission. Decisions presented themselves much more clearly because we knew whom we had to reach and whom we had to impress.

Know Your Target

Another group you must not overlook is single adults. These people have always been bypassed by the majority of churches. If a person is single and in school, the church has a plan for his or her life. If that person is not a student, it gets a little more diffi-cult to find ministry targeted toward him or her. If that person is single-all-over-again (divorced, widowed, etc.), few notice his or her needs. Why not target a church toward single adults? This is what I did in 1971. I found a need and filled it—as a result, growth came easily. My motives were partly self-serving. I had inherited a very small building from my denomination. We had no staff and little money. I simply could not imagine running a full-service Christian education program. Realizing that most singles did not have kids made me consider their needs over those of married people. Furthermore, I realized that singles do not have a lot of time commitments and are available for min-istry. This made them even more attractive.

Once I discovered that other churches did not seem to know that singles existed, I was off to the races. We set a goal to have the largest singles group in our part of Southern California within one year of our birth, thereby also meeting the need for greatness. When singles found out that we cared about them, they came in droves. I began praying for our singles to fall in love with each other, thus creating families. Talking about this part of my prayer life further enhanced church growth. It was later that the light went on and I saw how this affected tithes and offerings. Singles usually bring home one income (tithe check) per person, whereas families often account for one income spread over three, four or more people. Almost by accident we built a force capable of funding and executing rapid church multiplication from the base of a lone congregation.

Differentiate Yourself from All Others

I preach without a pulpit because our church does not want to appear liturgical. Actually, I do not preach—I teach from a large hardback Bible with lots of footnotes and helps. I use the big Bible because it looks more like a book than a religious icon. I want people to value the Scriptures above all else that we do. We meet between services at round tables under umbrellas in a courtyard. The setup resembles a large Starbucks. This is intentional on our part because our target audience for evangelism is still under 30. We have also put in place other factors that set us apart. We work hard to look and feel different from any other church in our community.

When every organization looks pretty much the same, people will revert to founding dates or size as differentiators of credibility. In other words, they will trust the oldest or the biggest churches long before they will pay attention to the new church planter in town. You must break the mold if you are to thrive.

You have to differentiate yourself to tap into the imagination of the people you are trying to evangelize. Successful people in the mainstream marketplace know and use this principle. Peter Drucker insists that organizations that thrive are those that are willing to abandon everything *conventional* for something better.[3] McDonald's *invented* fast food. Toys-R-Us virtually created the big-box retail industry. The Body Shop made an art form out of bathroom utility items. Each one found success by ignoring the past for a better, although unconventional method of product delivery. Their differences were often quite pragmatic. They simply took a fresh approach and packed it with enthusiasm. McDonald's did not invent the hamburger; it just found a new exciting way to package a meal and get it into the customers' hands faster than anyone else.

If anything, the traditions of the past are friends of innovators, whether it is in business or in the church. Traditionalists quickly go on the attack. They predict the demise and fault the methods of anything fresh and different. Through their protests detractors provide an extra layer of publicity—a buzz that enhances the new venture's standing among the people it is trying to reach.

Talk about differentiation! Jesus' message drastically differed from both the theologically conservative Pharisees and their liberal counterparts, the Sadducees. Nicodemus admitted that the Pharisees acknowledged Jesus' miracles but disbelieved His words (see John 3:1-9). The Sadducees bought into neither the miracles He performed nor His teachings. This rejection extended to the apostles. Paul's message and style offended the synagogue rulers in nearly every city in which he preached. Yet the same message sparked interest in the multitudes who eventually populated the Early Church. Notice that Early Church leaders did not differentiate themselves for the sake of gathering a crowd or just being different. However, they never held back from doing the right or obvious thing just because it broke with tradition. Both their message and their courage set them apart from their peers.

Look at the fastest-growing churches today. They all have characteristics that set them apart from the average church in their communities. They also differ from each other—which is a good reason why you should not copy them. You should think through your vision, your target group and the needs of the people you want to reach with the gospel. Devise a unique strategy that will get the attention and gain the hearts of the people in your community.

> **Helpful Hint:** Competition simply does not belong in the Church. If you keep it from your thinking, then you will be free of the church across the freeway or around the corner. This freedom will allow you to see needs that they are not meeting and reach people they have overlooked. Competition between churches breeds clones. Partnership among churches fosters creativity and frees congregations from imitating one another.

Start with a Crowd

Church-growth scholar and cell-church builder Dale Galloway has given me wonderful insights into ministry. He once observed that the truly great churches in our country nearly all started with more than 200 persons on the opening day. In his thinking, critical mass is achieved with a crowd of 200. Fall short of that mark and it is not likely that you will ever grow truly large.

His statement got my attention. At Hope Chapel, we have often opened the doors to a new church with little more than a core team of disciples. Looking to Jesus as a model, we took for granted that a dozen or so dedicated people would eventually grow into a much larger congregation. While we have had much success at planting churches, Galloway's remarks have moved us to reprioritize our efforts toward building a much larger audience on opening day. We still build a core team and meet as a church in the smaller group, but we work harder to start off with a bang when the church goes public.

This is more a change of approach than attitude for me. We will still build great small churches in small communities or for smaller demographic groups in huge cities. What I learned from Galloway was the benefit of spending more money to announce that first Sunday meeting. His message is that a bigger bang at the beginning makes for smoother sailing down the line.

Advertise Your Church

If you are going to reach critical mass, you must move beyond a small core group to a viable congregation—whatever the actual number might be. This will require effective communication. Before you choose your methods of communication, you need to have a broad understanding of advertising and what it can do for you. What worked for one church plant will not necessarily work for another. All churches are different. Leaders are unlike each other. Each city has its own quirks. Furthermore, the cost of advertising varies. Cost differentials dictate what can be done effectively from one community to another.

Television and radio broadcast their message over a huge area. Newspapers are more specific since they offer their words to a narrower range of consumers. A telephone campaign or postcard mailing focuses on a narrowly defined list of potential clients. Telephone calls and postcard mailings are means of *narrowcasting* while television and radio are examples of *broadcasting*. Newspapers fall somewhere in between. Word-of-mouth contact is narrowcasting at its interactive best. Broadcasters work with huge budgets. People with less money usually resort to narrowcasting.

Count the Cost per Contact

A message telecast to a huge city is an expensive proposition. The same communication will cost less to broadcast on a small-town station. Yet the cost *per contact* is actually much lower in the larger city than it is in the town. Broadcasting to a large audience affords an efficiency of scale that cannot be matched in smaller markets. This means that while it costs more to broadcast to a large audience, it actually costs less for each person you confront.

You will have to determine if television is worth the per-person cost in your community.

Postcards or door hangers cost about the same per contact in both small markets and the big city. They also cost more per contact than television does in either setting. This difference shows how narrowcasting is far more costly than broadcasting. However, postcards are often more attractive because you can limit or increase the number you distribute, depending upon the funds available to you. Thus, while your cost per contact is higher, your bottom line may be lower. With the postcard, you can also target specific neighborhoods. A postcard can go to the immediate area surrounding the church and to every person who visited over a certain period of time. Finally, the postcard will actually be seen and handled (if only to be discarded) by every recipient. The recipient interacts with you when he or she touches the card and decides to read it or throw it away. Every interaction works to your benefit. At the very least, a postcard puts the name of your church before a large number of people in your community.

When we started Hope Chapel in Southern California, we used the local daily newspaper and flyers stuck in screen doors as our primary means of communication. The newspaper gave us broadcast coverage within the local community rather than all over Los Angeles County. The fliers gave us the focus of narrowcasting without the expense of the postal service, since we distributed them ourselves. Self-distribution also created a role for volunteers.

Spread Your Message Through Word of Mouth

You have heard it before, but it is still correct: Word of mouth is the best form of advertising. Another tried-and-true slogan boasts "The best things in life are free." The best things may be free, but word-of-mouth advertising is not one of them. If people have good things to say about you, it is because you made a strong investment in their opinion. You do this by offering great teaching, wonderful worship and intense personal service. You can also do it by spending money on advertising and communications.

The Crossroads church built a dramatic newspaper campaign to introduce themselves. In my California church, we gave away 20,000 copies of a book addressing the needs of the community. In Hawaii, our unique church location got people talking. Rick Warren of Saddleback Community Church in California spent 10 percent of his early budgets on advertising, mostly through direct mail.

Whatever approach you take, this question should drive your efforts: How can I get people talking? Every communication should support the personal evangelistic efforts of your core team and growing body of members.

CHOOSE YOUR ADVERTISING TOOLS

Before you make any decisions about advertising make sure you know what tools are available to you and the return you can expect from each one. There are several good books on marketing and advertising that you should read. The one book that every church planter should own is the *Guerrilla Marketing Handbook* by Jay Conrad Levinson. After reading it, you should have a basic grasp of the tools that are available to you. You will also have enough of a feel for marketing to know which other books you might like to pick up at a local bookstore. Get a feel for the marketing and advertising worlds before you recruit help. A little knowledge gives you leverage when someone comes up with bright ideas that do not quite fit your purpose or style.

As part of your homework, check among your friends to see who has expertise in this crucial area. Build a team. Be willing to spend a significant portion of your budget to get the word out. Do not rely solely on the ideas I am about to give you. These can be discussion starters, but do not get hung up on *either* broadcasting *or* narrowcasting. You will do better using both tools in concert and finding out what works best in the community where you are about to plant a church.

> **Helpful Hint:** Above all else, differentiate your church from all others in your communication efforts.

Take Advantage of Television

You can get free time on public-service television. It is surprisingly effective, but hardly practical for a church that has not yet held a meeting. However, I know one pastor who designed a half-hour special as an invitation to a new church. The format contained music, cuts of him preaching, testimonies and five minutes of the pastor describing his vision. The entire broadcast carried subtitles giving directions to the new church. The type crawled continually across the bottom of the screen. He ran the broadcast several times a day on both public-access and commercial television for two weeks.

Radio Gets Results

For six months before moving to Hawaii we aired a daily radio broadcast in Honolulu on a Christian station. The tapes were of my preaching in California. Shortly before opening the new church, we announced the new church at the end of each daily broadcast. We invited listeners to a potluck dinner hosted by our core team.

As soon as we moved off the beach we used the radio broadcast to announce our grand opening. For this we only advertised a phone number, so we could speak with anyone who was interested. As a way to save money, the advertisements were placed in the final minutes of our daily broadcasts. The number connected to a second line in my house. Callers were surprised and pleased when they found themselves talking to the voice they listened to on the radio. Once services actually began, the advertisements turned to an invitation for people with pain in their lives to come visit. They ended with the words "We promise to love you . . . as is!" We took some heat for the grammar, but the message was effective.

If you cannot afford a typical 30-minute time slot for a preaching program, then try a shorter version. Many stations will sell you time for a series of 30-second or one-minute thought-for-the-day messages. This is a great way to introduce yourself as a preacher.

You can get free exposure on radio, too, but the approach varies greatly from community to community and station to station. All stations, Christian and mainstream, air public service announcements (PSAs) for free. Find out who the PSA directors are at the stations in your community. Write up 15- and 30-second spots. Do not worry about how slick they are; just get in all of the information—the station will likely change the copy anyway. You can submit material for your church opening and any special events, but do not try to get them to announce your service every week. Be sure to end with your telephone number. Usually stations require PSAs to be submitted four to six weeks in advance. Honor this lead time, and you are more likely to have yours used on the air.

Another way to get radio coverage is through a local talk show. Christian stations with hosts who air their shows live are always looking for a local angle. This is where your distinction can be emphasized. If you are like every other church that exists or has attempted to come to town, the host is not likely to be interested. But if you can catch the imagination of the host, then you have taken a huge step toward raising interest in the wider community. Find out who the producer of the show is, and be careful to follow his or her guidelines—these will vary from station to station. Also, be patient. Producers historically take a long time to reply to queries, and their priorities are often bumped by current events.

Use the Friendly Skies

I used the mystique of travel to build a long-distance core team before planting the church in Hawaii. As we gleaned contacts through the radio we began leaking the idea of a new church long before our public announcement. In addition to the core team at home, we built a group that met every week in Hawaii. I would visit once a month for two days, bringing current news of our plans to the group. The relatively small cost of the travel paid big dividends. Not only did people feel tied to the group on the mainland, they fed the grapevine in Hawaii about the guy flying in from California each month to plant a new church. Because our activities were still officially secret, the gossip magnified our every move. We reaped huge exposure for the price of seven airline tickets.

Be Selective in Your Use of Newspaper Ads

Newspaper advertisements are effective for a church that frequently changes meeting places because you can telegraph last-minute information to your entire constituency. But I do not recommend them as attention grabbers unless you are willing and able to spend a lot of money. This is because the church with the largest ad gets the most attention. The only time this might not be true is if the largest advertisement is boring. If you are up against boring ads, you can grab attention and imagination with clever communication. But if the largest ads are good, your cleverness can backfire, leaving you appearing odd in the eyes of those you want to address.

Do not try running church-meeting advertisements in the sports pages or in the business section. If you advertise in the paper, you will likely get your best results if you address those people already in search of spiritual truth. They use the church page as a directory in their search. Money spent in the other sections of the paper is generally wasted in comparison to the effectiveness of the church page or religion section of the Saturday newspaper. I learned this through months of expensive efforts with clever ads in the sports section. I know that some churches have gotten results by advertising special events or grand openings in the entertainment section, but we have not seen that at Hope Chapel. In fact, we ran very expensive advertisements in the sports section for months and saw very little results.

Helpful Hint: Introduce yourself to the religion editor at your local paper. He or she may write an article about you or at least include you in the announcements section. Do not overlook the weeklies. Many people in the community read these free papers. A married couple in Huntington Beach, California, read an article about Bill White's church plant, Surfer's Chapel. They came to make fun of it, ended up accepting Jesus and now are on the Surfer's Chapel core team.

Take Your Message to the Movies

One of the principal tenets of advertising is name identity. You want to get your church name in front of as many people in your target groups as possible. Placing slides in movie theaters provides a good way to connect with unchurched people. Those who would not find you on the church page in the newspaper will not be able to avoid your message, as they crunch their popcorn. This form of communication is fairly inexpensive. It also involves an extra element of surprise and innovation. No one expects to hear from a church as they wait for the opening of an R-rated film. This aura of the unexpected will only last until theaters become a common place for churches to try to reach people.

Bus Benches Can Spread the Word

We ran signs on bus benches in California. This kind of advertising is not allowed in Hawaii, or we would still do it. Parked everywhere, these are great places to hang your logo, phone number and web address. They reinforce your members' attempts at evangelism, too. When someone hears the gospel and is invited to church, they will respond favorably to a church they think they know, even if they only know your name. We tested this. An unchurched person would say, "That's a good church—I've heard about that church." When we asked how they heard, our bus benches would inevitably comprise part, if not all, of their answer.

Take Advantage of the Internet and E-Mail

Fax machines preceded the Internet by a generation. Never a household tool in America, they grew as common as refrigerators in Japan. For a decade some Japanese pastors faxed, and thus broadcast, announcements to their congregations. Some published midweek Bible studies by fax machine. Then they got instant messaging on cell phones. Now they are more connected than ever. The Japanese saw both electronic implements as opportunities to carry their message to their people.

In the meantime, the Internet sneaked up on the American church. We bought PCs while the Japanese were buying fax machines. We use our cell phones to talk while the Japanese use theirs for e-mail. We went online while they did not. There is another difference, too. Unlike the Japanese, we communicate *passively* with our people. We design church websites to look much like a sign on the front of the building expanded to include brochures describing how the church functions. This is useful information, and the Internet is a great place to display it. But it is still passive. A person has to want the information badly enough to go to your passive site. This means he or she must first know it is there. That is the rub. How do you get the viewer to visit your website in the first place?

By joining e-mail to the web, you can communicate aggressively. Create a single-page addendum to announce an event. Dress it up with pictures. E-mail your audience a short message that involves them to the page and contains a link to get there. This way you take the information to them instead of waiting for them to discover it. You can target your mailings to your members using your database. E-mail-driven Internet announcements can carry a lot of color with none of the cost attached to printed material. They also position your people to pass on your message at the click of their mouse. You will multiply your audience.

Spamming people with unwanted e-mail is obviously something you do not want to do. But we have found that our own people appreciate e-mail messages from their church family. In addition, they can be very judicious in passing the message along to people in their own circle of influence. You may want to instruct your congregation on how and when to send along church e-mail messages to others.

Do not just send advertisements for events. Helpful information carefully packaged makes a great addition to a website. We do this regularly with that hope that the information will appear on the screens of unchurched people in our community. For instance, in the aftermath of the September 11 attack on the World Trade Center, we published a web sheet called "How to Talk to Kids About Tragedy." Our people passed that link to thousands of non-Christians. The information equipped them to share their faith but from a low-key perspective.

Look for Creative Ways to Communicate

The first time my wife and I planted a church, we did so with almost no resources. We were given an empty building and $600. To this we added our personal savings. A goofy idea came knocking at our door a month later. We would ask a philanthropist named W. Clement Stone for 20,000 copies of David Wilkerson's book *The Cross and the Switchblade*. The book documents God's power to deliver heroin addicts in New York City from their poison. It also described the birth of Teen Challenge treatment centers, a project funded by Stone. Wilkerson's message was pertinent to just about everyone, as the drug revolution was still in its infancy. Fearful parents of young children were as interested as adults who were trying to shake off a recently acquired habit.

Mr. Stone gave us the money to buy the books. When we requested the books there were fewer than 20 people in our church. When the books arrived we numbered just about 100 persons. That meant giving away 200 books per member. It took just two weeks to deliver those books to people in the workplace, on beaches, outside of school buildings, in jails and in any other place you could imagine. A sticker adorned each book, offering my home phone number as a help line for people battling drug addiction. My phone nearly wore out in the next six weeks, but the book put us on the map. Such a project could do the same for you. Why not put together a short book on some subject that troubles your intended audience. It could be about getting along with the opposite sex, prayer, money management or how to conquer fear. Include a chapter detailing your mission and self-publish it. For about a dollar a book you can introduce yourself and your church to the people you want to reach. A reader investing a couple of hours in your message is quite likely to join you on your crusade to bettering the world.

Flyers Can Reach Your Community

Because we started the first church with almost no funds we could not afford much for printing. Commercially set type was expensive. Therefore, we used an electric typewriter and rub-on letters. Tacky as they were, the flyers we created were effective. We hand delivered the *Waves of Faith Newsletter* to every home in our city. Each edition went to 200 homes immediately surrounding our church plus 1,800 additional families. Then we kept publishing new editions until we had hand delivered 13,000 copies over all. This gave us depth in our immediate community while gaining some access to the whole city. Being able to brag about touching every house in town also inspired our members to share their faith. But the real success came from those 200 homes. We eventually planted several churches with leaders we mentored from that immediate neighborhood.

Know your demographics. Our church targets younger people. But on one neighborhood blitz we hung literature on a few thousand doors in an older, better-established neighborhood in Kaneohe. For the following two weeks we were flooded with Japanese-American grandmothers visiting our church for the first time. Most did not like our loud music and youthful atmosphere. We had wasted their time and our own efforts by our sloppy planning.

Use the Mail

You can buy beautiful commercially prepared color postcards designed to invite people to your church. They are inexpensive and shine with quality. This is a great way to announce your presence. If you are mailing, you should hit the same neighborhood each time to build your church's identity in the minds of the residents. Spreading your bets all over town like I did with my flyers helps breed vision in your members. But it is repeated communication that brings in new people. Again, target specific neighborhoods. Who are you trying to reach? Where do they live? This is narrowcasting with strength.

Go Door-to-Door

Like postcards, door hangers are great tools to narrowcast your message. It may be a little harder to find a printer to produce them, but they are great for involving lots of people in a community effort. Ringing doorbells just does not work for most people. Folks inside the house think you are a salesman or cult leader. Church members are usually terrified at the thought of talking with strangers. Hanging a slip of paper over a doorknob is easier and can mobilize your people behind your vision. They will end up talking to some strangers—the folks washing their cars or picking up their mail. They will make friends along the way and invite them to church. The results will surprise and motivate your entire team.

Door hangers do three things for you. First, they cost less than postcards. Sixty percent of the cost of postcards is in postage. Second, they effectively bring people in your front doors. The third benefit is priceless. Seeing results of their own efforts motivates your current members to share their faith among family and friends. Now you are feeding the word-of-mouth process.

Make Your Vehicle an Advertising Tool

While I was writing this book, I met a man who accepted Jesus Christ as his Savior. He had come to our church after seeing bumper stickers we hung on our cars. He had asked a friend the meaning behind her bumper sticker that reads, "Hope Chapel Kaneohe Bay." The friend gave him her own testimony, shared the gospel with him and invited him to church. He accepted the Lord the week of his first visit. This is a common story in our congregation.

The sticker *cannot* bring a person to church or to the Lord. It *can* place a member in a position to answer questions about his or her faith. Answering questions for an interested party is lots easier than preaching to skeptics.

Do Not Forget the Personal Touch

Another tool that has proven to be effective is a printed personal invitation the size of a business card. These cards should look like the small advertisements published by coffee shops or dance clubs in your neighborhood. Challenge your members to give away 12 each month. They can leave them in restaurants along with generous tips or give them to strangers they meet almost anywhere. Do this yourself so you are a part of the outreach action. Share your stories and the ones you hear from your people. You will be surprised at the creativity of your people and the effectiveness of printed communication. The card will do more than you ask of it. Your team will find themselves talking to others about the gospel.

Gather and Protect Momentum

Look to create momentum when you plan your kickoff. Do not mistake opening day as the end of your efforts. It is truly just the starting point. You should think like a football coach who is planning for opening day. Your first series of plays will be foundational to all that you do. But they only provide a foundation.

You need to ask yourself several questions: How will you build on whatever gains you make with that first strike? What kind of outreach will keep the church growing during those first few crucial months? What will you teach the people, and how will your teaching contribute to further growth?

I like to arm people with truth and tools. When planting a new congregation, I teach through Philippians for the first four weeks. Teaching verse by verse through this short book establishes the church as a fountain of God's Word. It also lifts people spiritually.

After Philippians I teach through Acts, focusing on the nature and calling of our church. While in Acts, we encounter our call to local and world outreach. We learn the role of the Holy Spirit in our worship and our works. We build church structure and learn the importance of home groups. Peter's sermon on Pentecost helps us understand this last point.

In our first months as a church we discover discipleship and mentoring as Philip and Stephen progress from deacons to effective preachers. The point here is to tie the teaching to the structure of the church and to plant both in the hearts of the people. While outreach efforts bring people in the front door, the teaching molds them into a missionary force as they return to their daily lives. The entire package results in sustained evangelism, church growth and momentum in the spiritual life of the congregation.

CHURCH PLANTER'S CHECKLIST

1. What is there about your vision or style that could be described as great?
2. What could you do to raise the greatness quotient?
3. Define your primary mission field.
4. List 10 things that you could do to differentiate your church from all others (keep them practical and biblical).
5. Arrange the advertising tools I have suggested in this chapter in priority order in terms of how they fit your community and your budget.
6. Find out if there is anyone in your network who has experience in advertising or marketing.

7. Check prices and begin devising a simple campaign announcing your new church.

Notes

1. Tom Peters, *The Tom Peters Seminar* (New York: Vintage Books, 1994), p. 106.
2. Ralph Moore, *Friends: The Key to Reaching Generation X* (Ventura, CA: Regal Books, 2001), pp. 33-34.
3. Peter F. Drucker, "The New Society of Organizations," *Harvard Business Review* (Sept.-Oct. 1992), p. 98.

PART 3

PLANTING THE
New Church

CHAPTER 13

STRUCTURE:
CAN YOU BUILD A CHURCH THAT FLEXES AS IT GROWS?

Every church needs internal structure just as every building needs a frame. Church planters sometimes postpone making plans for the *shape* of the church until after patterns have formed without any specific design in mind. I made this mistake in the first church I planted. You do not have to repeat the error. You can design an organizational structure before you start. As you map your church, try to achieve a pattern so flexible that it can fit any size assembly of believers. The Bible contains such a plan.

FOLLOW THE NEW TESTAMENT'S ARCHITECTURAL BLUEPRINT

Luke gave us more in the book of Acts than a random account of the first-century Church. He wrote with purpose. He penned a record of the Jerusalem congregation and its most successful avenue of penetration into the Mediterranean world. This historical narrative features the original apostles, the evangelistic success of those scattered by the persecution associated with Saul of Tarsus and the driving energy of Paul.

Luke's work is not a comprehensive history. He could have followed the trail into Ethiopia. Or he could have noted all of the details surrounding the believers who had fled from Jerusalem during the persecution after Stephen's death (see Acts 11:19). Instead, he wrote a training manual for the believers who would come later. His description of the Early Church is a prototype for us to *emulate*. It is not a description of a primitive attempt for us to *improve* upon over time. It is a strategy for the ages. A great book that links this strategic description to the direction of the Holy Spirit is C. Peter Wagner's *Acts of the Holy Spirit*.[1]

Look at What They Did in Jerusalem

With these thoughts in mind, let's look at the architecture of the church in Jerusalem after the day of Pentecost. The apostles were scrambling. They lived through the logistical trauma of 2,600 percent growth in one day. There would be no more Upper-Room meetings for their congregation. They needed more space.

Believers began to meet in the Temple in a place called Solomon's Porch. They also gathered in the homes of the newly converted (see Acts 2:41-47; 3:11; 5:12). They would have needed more houses than those of the original congregation on the morning of Pentecost if you project about 10 persons in each home meeting. They would also have needed at least eight meetings in Solomon's porch to accommodate the original 120 plus the converts from the Day of Pentecost. Even eight meetings project no growth at a time when the Lord added to their number on a daily basis. These early Christians obviously had to hustle to keep up with the Holy Spirit.

Leaders were certainly in short supply. Eleven apostles plus Matthias could have easily handled the large-group meetings, but hundreds of lay leaders would have been necessary to complement them in the home meetings. Training would have been informal based on the model of Jesus' investment in the lives of the original Twelve.

This is the example left to us as the best way to operate a growing congregation. The key elements are large-group meetings run by well-discipled leaders, small groups where fellowship has integrity and the rapid deployment of leaders.

BREAK OFF INTO SMALL GROUPS

The relationship between large public meetings and small, intimate support teams is crucial in Luke's writing. It is also paramount in modern churches. When I planted my first church we attracted several people already leading small groups in other churches. Soon we were a collection of randomly developed cells. Eventually, most of the groups died because the leaders lacked training and because we provided them with no unifying direction.

We hit a point of crisis when we reached a weekend attendance of about 600 people. We had already aborted two attempts to kick off small groups.[2] Part of our problem with leadership development was my own sense of inadequacy. I assumed that I had to offer leaders some sort of deeper spiritual experience than we enjoyed in our other meetings and training venues. I just did not have it in me. The other problem was that we saw small groups as an addendum to the church. We ran three regular events each week with the assumption that everyone would want to attend. There was a Sunday-morning service, a Sunday-evening Bible study and a midweek prayer service. Small groups meant people had to attend a fourth meeting each week. Only the extremely faithful would come. Of course none of the other meetings was as popular as the flagship Sunday-morning celebration. The midweek meeting drew only 1/10th as many people. And the home groups just were not happening.

One of our daughter churches solved this problem of over-scheduling. In the wake of their success, we conjured up a plan to train leaders and operate small groups instead of our midweek Bible study. It was an instant success.

We replaced other services with home meetings, as well. Attendance exploded with a 500-percent growth in one week. Abandoning our midweek prayer service for a worship/Bible study/prayer/fellowship format struck a chord of need in our people. These groups broke from tradition in two ways. First, at that time the church generally did not expect believers to tack on an extra meeting each week or to abandon any midweek meeting. The second break from church-as-usual was what took place in the small-group meeting. We reviewed the past weekend's teaching. Our people could discuss the message, ask questions and offer their own opinions and spiritual responses to what had been taught. The new format also allowed people *without* the gift of teaching to take leadership roles in the meeting. We discovered that more people have pastoral care skills than enjoy a teaching gift. Leaders suddenly became plentiful.

Leadership development solved itself in two stages. During the first few weeks we would gather all the small-group leaders on Sunday afternoons to brainstorm discussion questions rooted in the weekend sermon. Those questions unified the church and clarified the message in the minds of the leaders. Later I began publishing questions along with the printed sermon notes. At that point we moved to purchasing books for each cell leader. We would read the books independently, discussing what we had learned in the corporate meeting. Leadership training simplified itself. It also moved us forward as we had our entire leadership team reading the same material at the same time.

Get Ready to Manage Your Cells, Congregation and Celebration

During the 1980s, I read a lot about cells, congregation and celebration as the basic building blocks for church development. At that time, the trend ran toward discussion of the cell, or small group, without much emphasis on the midsized congregation or the larger weekend worship celebration. Today much more is written about megachurches. Hence, the celebration service gets most of the ink without many words devoted to smaller groups. In spite of what we read, every church, if it grows large enough, will contain all three. You do not choose whether you will have these different groups. You only decide how you will manage them.

I define cells as groups of three to 20 people, knowing that attendance becomes sporadic at the larger end of the scale. Congregations are groups of about 20 to 120 people. Celebration occurs when more than 120 people gather.

The names imply the purpose or at least the nature of the group. Cells usually focus on some specific task or on the needs of individual members. Congregations also congregate around a task. The focus of congregations can include upholding the honor of the church in a softball game. Choirs are excellent examples of the congregational group. Missions teams often function as congregations. Celebration meetings are times of jubilant expression. Members come to fulfill individual needs and rejoice in the support they gain by meeting with a larger group. The size of the celebration reinforces personal faith and feelings toward God.

Each group has its place and will occur naturally as people get to know each other, give to each other's personal needs and establish spiritual agendas. But organically driven groups present a problem. How do you balance spontaneity with strategic purpose? How do you keep the direction of various groups focused on a unifying vision? Let spontaneity rule and you abdicate leadership. Yet if you attempt to control every startup, you restrict and perhaps kill growth. You need to find a balance.

Beware of the Focus Breaker

It is not as difficult as you might think to achieve balance between spontaneity and purposeful leadership. Just keep an eye on your congregation gatherings—those are where the potential focus breakers reside. Momentum can build around an outside agenda, which could then threaten the vision of senior leadership. Individual cells are too small to influence the overall mission of the church. Celebration meetings provide an anchor for the vision, purpose and mission of the core leadership team. Steer your congregations so they support what you put forth in the celebration gatherings. Fail them as a central leader, and you will invite chaos.

You must be sure that each new congregation embraces the overall purpose and mission of your church. The best congregational leaders are people with their own driving agendas, but sometimes these can be hidden. Usually these people are fired up by an act of the Holy Spirit. They come to you that way rather than as a product of your red-hot leadership. Do not view their agenda or their passion as a threat. Instead find a way to position their agenda strategically within the parameters of your own. Keep them accountable to you and your vision. Devise tools that train them in the overall direction of the church. Then give them permission to dream big and accomplish great things in the name of the Lord and your church. Freedom within boundaries is what you want to achieve. Connect them with other people and the resources they need to accomplish their task. Finally, give them so much credit for their accomplishments that others are inspired to follow in their footsteps.

Focus is the key. It will make or break your relationship with these natural leaders. If they can work within your vision, you will build a great team. If not, dissolve the relationship as soon as you realize it cannot work. What you do not want is to constantly force bit and bridle into the mouth of a wild horse. If the person will work with you, give him or her a measure of freedom.

Set Up a Framework That Encourages Growth
At every level, build systems that will give groups the freedom to multiply. As I have already noted, flexibility is an integral ingredient.

> **Helpful Hint:** Do not position yourself as the hole in the hourglass through which every decision must flow.

Leaders should pick their own apprentices and replacements. They should determine when to hand off a new group and who will lead it. You are a weak pastor if you must know, personally, every cell leader in your church. Trust comes through relationship. You know someone—you trust that person. They know the next person—they trust them. The second-generation leader automatically merits your trust because you trust the person who trusts in them.

Congregations will rise spontaneously out of the hearts of visionary people in your midst. Can you imagine yourself possessing a burning desire to locate a decrepit fire engine for an impoverished and recently burned-out village in northern Mexico? Would you, as pastor, assemble a huge team to restore the vehicle down to the red paint, pumps, drive train and shiny brass? Would you lead a caravan of 200 people to deliver the fire engine after four years of effort? I would not. Yet I saw a congregation leap forward with growth and enthusiasm because one pastor allowed another man in his church to pursue just such a passion. The church had a strong missionary presence in Mexico. That made it easy for the people to congregate around the fire engine project, and it fit in with the overall mission of the church. The pastor provided lots of freedom, but within certain parameters. That is what you will need to do in order to add a layer of spontaneous excitement to your congregation. More congregations with goal-oriented missions equals more people thrilled about serving God.

At a celebration level, you want to think of multiplication right from the start. Build service schedules with multiplication in mind. In the West, people like to go to church early on Sunday. Lots of churches schedule their primary worship celebration for 9 A.M. This is a mistake if you plan to multiply that meeting. A move from 9 A.M. to an 8 A.M. and 10 A.M. format requires that you break up the schedule of the entire membership. It would be much better to start at either 8 A.M. or 10 A.M., adding another service later. I do not recommend that you split your celebration meeting into two equal-sized groups through a schedule change. You will be much happier if you start a second meeting without a lot of fanfare and let it gain numbers over time. Momentum is precious and will be lost when a service suddenly only has half as many people in attendance.

Draw People Toward the Center

You need to devise a system capable of moving someone from a first-time visitor all the way into the core of your church family.

What will you offer first-time visitors? How will you draw them into personal patterns of growth? I like Rick Warren's concentric circles he uses to describe the relationship of any individual to the local church. In his book *The Purpose Driven Church* he describes how people start as members of the community. They join the crowd of attendees the day they visit for the first time. He casts members who have joined the church as the congregation. The "committed" are mature members who have found a place to serve. The core is made up of lay ministers.[3]

The core of a church extends to the board and pastors, especially in churches that recruit and train their pastoral staff from within. Since every church attracts far more first timers than it keeps as regular members, carefully maintaining this pathway to growth is crucial to the health of the church and of every individual it touches.

Find the Transition Points
If you accept Warren's circles as a model, you need to look at the transition points between each of the circles. What moves a person from the crowd into the congregation? Some movement happens almost without effort, as some people come greatly motivated toward intimacy with God and His Church. Perhaps an acceleration of this work of the Spirit is what separates revivals from normal operating circumstances, but building only on the motivation of first-time visitors will only allow very slow growth; it might even reverse your momentum. You need to be as aggressive in moving newcomers to the center of church life as you are at advertising in the community.

We give first-time visitors a free recording of the weekend message and a packet of spiritual formation goodies if they return an information form attached to our weekly bulletin. They also receive an informal note from me and an invitation to attend our Taste of Hope barbecue. The food is great and plentiful. They get to meet the staff and hear our history, vision, values and purpose. Many who come to the barbecues sign our membership book. This three-hour event also helps place about one third of those attending into entry-level ministry positions. Nearly 50 percent will go directly from the barbecue to one of our cell groups, which we call MiniChurches, or other small-group meetings.

Any first-time visitor who indicates that he or she has made a decision to become a Christian receives another recorded teaching. This one gives them basic information on how to pray and introduces them to several Scriptures dealing with love and forgiveness. It also describes the ministries offered by the church and tells how we can serve them, individually. These people receive a call and are invited to attend an eight-week class called "Starting Fresh with God." At the end of the class most of the attendees join one of our small groups or some ministry team. We also offer a second midweek class working through the book of Romans using a text called *How to Be a Christian Without Being Religious*.[4] Further advancement into the core comes at the personal invitation of people already serving on the team. We call that process succession management.

Prepare Leadership Team Replacements
Each person in ministry recruits his or her own team from among his or her followers and arranges for his or her own replacement. Most recruitment is done through the natural course of friendship. Theoretically every person on your leadership team has his or her replacement ready to go at a moment's notice.

Members of small groups who show leadership ability are recruited as apprentice leaders. When the group multiplies itself, one of those apprentices will lead the original group while the leader who recruited him or her plants a new group. At Hope

Chapel, we produce great training events but reserve them for those people who have already begun to serve. We try to avoid wholesale announcements for help, even in freshly planted churches. Putting the transition from spectator to worker into the hands of our leaders gives us a huge cadre of recruiters.

Succession management works at the very core of our church, too. We recruit pastors from the ranks of small-group leaders. If people can start and successfully lead three small groups (not all at one time), we assume they have pastoral gifts. They know our values and our system. They have demonstrated fruitfulness and faithful service. Our practice prevents many hiring mistakes. Homegrown church planters produce results.

The people we hire, we also train—incessantly. Full- and part-time pastoral staff members attend biweekly Tuesday evening meetings called The Pastor Factory. We study about four books each year. Each person does the same reading assignment and comes prepared to discuss or even to teach it. Leading these meetings gives me an opportunity, as senior pastor, to directly disciple my staff. Each of them leads a similar group of volunteer small-group pastors on the alternating Tuesdays. This is a discipleship training school that never takes a recess. A person graduates only when he or she moves to a different city or leaves to plant a church.

COUNT THE NUMBERS THAT COUNT

I entered pastoral ministry at a time when it was fashionable to discount the importance of numbers in any discussion of church health or growth. This was an overreaction against people who liked to hold the size of their congregation over the heads of their peers. However, numbers are important to any measure of progress.

Consider These Three Important Numbers

There are 3 numbers in the Bible that can mark success or failure in the life of any pastor. These are 3, 11 and 120. Three—
because you need a Peter, James and John in your life. Jesus had
a team of 3, and you must emulate Him if you are ever to build
anything solid enough to outlast your lifetime. Eleven suggests
that each of your 3 should have 3 team members of their own.
This would, of course, add up to 12. But you will probably have
a Judas in your midst, knocking you down to 11.

The 120 is a little trickier. If Jesus left behind a congregation
of 120 on the Day of Pentecost, then we ought to measure success by that number. We should never worry about reaching
5,000 in attendance just because someone else did. If you pastor
40 people in a rural village, 120 makes a great and reachable lifelong goal. Weigh this in light of Luke's words: "Much is required
from those to whom much is given, and much more is required
from those to whom much more is given" (Luke 12:48). I believe
a person who pastors more than 120 people is obligated to take
a larger role in the Great Commission and to plant churches.
With several thousand the burden becomes much more apparent. Interestingly, we concurrently planted our first daughter
church and reached 120 in attendance at the mother church.
Our attendance averaged just 125 people each week. We gave
away 25 individuals that day, but the Lord had sent 50 newcomers to take their place. We always thought it was His way of saying, "Well done, good and faithful servants."

Meet People's Basic Needs

Everyone needs a fellowship circle—a place where everybody
knows his or her name. Involvement is the key to retaining those
who walk through the door of your new church. Both ministry
assignment and small-group membership will provide these
people with an outlet for their spiritual energies. Ministry tasks

provide purpose and fulfill the need to be *needed*. Small-group membership glues people together with a sense of belonging. It fulfills the *need to be recognized*. Involvement of both kinds will keep members fresh and happy. Spectators in church soon stagnate and create problems or drift away.

Create as many ministry assignments as you can. Work toward building identifiable positions in your church until 80 percent of your congregation has a post. For every 100 people try to define 80 jobs. This means you should break each position into three or four, creating a team with a leader and several apprentices. Find places for people to fit into your vision and purpose. Doing this will also spread the workload, easing the burden of recruitment.

Try to multiply small groups quickly enough that you have one group available for every 20 people in attendance. Press for 60 percent involvement. Groups can range from children's classes and recovery groups to prayer teams and Bible studies built around the weekend teaching. We even build our youth groups around David Yonggi Cho's celebration-cell model. Our young people run their own worship celebration and lead their home groups in the midweek. The important issue is to construct enough groups to meet the need for everyone to *belong*.

In nature, reproduction is the chief designator of maturity. The cells in your body form and grow and then reproduce. You do the same as a human being. If you structure it right, your church will follow this pattern—at every level.

CHURCH PLANTER'S CHECKLIST

1. Can you identify potential cell-group leaders within your core team?
2. Do you have seeds of congregations burning in the

hearts of the people who plan to go with you? List them and describe how you release them to ministry.

3. Write out a monthly schedule of events, including leadership training for your soon-to-be-born congregation.

4. Using Rick Warren's circles, describe transition tools to move people through each of the circles. Be original, do not just copy Rick. He does not pastor in your town.

Notes

1. C. Peter Wagner, *Acts of the Holy Spirit* (Ventura, CA: Regal Books, 2000).
2. Ralph Moore, *Friends: The Key to Reaching Generation X* (Ventura, CA: Regal Books, 2000), pp. 103-116.
3. Rick Warren, *The Purpose Driven Church* (Grand Rapids, MI: Zondervan Publishing House, 1995), p. 205.
4. Fritz Ridenour, *How To Be a Christian Without Being Religious* (Ventura, CA: Regal Books, 2002).

CHAPTER 14

WORSHIP:
HOW WILL YOU CREATE MEANINGFUL EXPERIENCES?

It took awhile for me to realize that I am a worship leader. I play no musical instruments. I sing so poorly that I must limit that exercise to large crowds or the shower. Nonetheless, I am the chief worship leader in my church—or so the people who make music inform me.

"The buck stops with you, pastor," one of our worship leaders told me. "Whatever we do must fit into your vision for this church, including worship." I responded that I know nothing about music. Another leader replied, "Music is only one part of worship. You should set the overall direction for worship. Then you can leave the music to us." This conversation actually took place a few years ago in my office. Afterwards I realized that I know plenty about the *results* of musical decisions although I cannot carry a tune. I had been harping at the worship teams over those results. We were always solving problems together, never casting vision. Through their remarks I discovered that I can delegate every part of the worship ministry *except* that of vision casting. That process defines a pastor as chief worship leader.

CAST A VISION FOR WORSHIP

Postmodern people crave genuineness. Since World War II our world has grown continuously more suspicious of itself. The self-appointed saviors of education and technology now lay battered by the wayside of life. Modernism itself proved to be just another false god. It made promises it could never fulfill. People growing up in a world filled with false promises crave authenticity. Even the most *irreligious* people are on a search for an experiential satisfaction for their souls. I have heard people say, "If I can feel it, it is real," and "If someone I trust experiences it, maybe I can believe it."

Extreme sports, E! and the Comedy Channel all tunnel into this lust for experiential reality. Your members will bring this kind of hunger to your church. They want to trust God because they can *feel* Him rather than feel Him because they trust Him. Your job is to create an environment where this can happen. You will make great strides toward capturing your audience if you explore and present the mystical side of Christianity to win the right to explain its ancient and modern truths.

I am not saying you should be the person at the keyboard or play the guitar. I know some pastors do that well, but I would always rather hand off ministry than have my hands on it. The pastor's job is different than playing an instrument.

As senior pastor, it is certainly your responsibility to help choose the overall style of music—it should relate closely to the culture of your target audience. You will approve the key individuals who will drive the worship experience. You also have the task of linking the worship experience and the talented musicians to your vision and to your understanding of God's Word.

At the same time, you will thrive if you delineate acceptable expressions of worship in the context of your local congregation. How far can people go in terms of interactive worship? Will it be appropriate to clap during praise songs? Can people raise their hands without being seen as fanatics? Are spontaneous prayers permissible during a time of quiet reflection? What about those people who always seem to want to stand through the entire worship time? What happens if the very young start to bounce around or dance in the aisles? In other words, your worship experience will be better defined once you establish the parameters of acceptable behavior. Hopefully you will use Scripture as a guide, as you decide what is right for your church.

Recognize the Importance of Worship
Worship has always been significant. The Westminster Shorter Catechism declares "Man's chief end is to glorify God, and to enjoy him forever."[1] The Scriptures make this clear: "You must do all for the glory of God" (1 Cor. 10:31). They also picture the God seeker saying, "God remains the strength of my heart; he is mine forever" (Ps. 73:26). This is heady stuff. God is the strength for which people hunger. Glorifying Him is the purpose for everybody's life whether he or she understands this truth or not. This means that your people *had better* connect with God enough to enjoy Him during service times. This enjoyment should follow them home. Then it should inspire them to *live* your teaching in a manner that brings Him glory. To do this, worship must be experiential and interactive. Be careful that you do not let

your worship program degenerate into entertainment. That may fill the seats, but I have never found that it is very effective at filling hearts. You will find people feeling God's presence when you keep worship important, relevant and experiential.

Your goal is to release faith in the hearts of your people. Jesus said the kingdom of heaven belongs to children and that "anyone who doesn't have their kind of faith will never get into the Kingdom of God" (Mark 10:15).

You may want to look to your children's programs for clues when you start to build interactivity into adult worship. One way they learn is when they make crafts. Another is by acting out lessons. Adult services could use a dose of this medicine.

Experience is the key to the heart of the postmodern world. Take a lesson from Islam. Regular and structured prayer times fuel Islamic fundamentalism in a world confused by too many choices. In some of our youngest and most vibrant evangelical churches, liturgical gestures have come off the sidelines and into the game. They move people into action through group recitation of prayer and responsive Scripture readings. Published sermon notes with lots of blanks to fill are suddenly popular. Group Bible marking is personally one of my favorite preaching tools. I regularly instruct my congregation where and what to write in the margins of their Bibles. I do this with the hope that their personal interaction with God's Word will increase. The people you face each week will want structured experiences to contain their faith, much like a cup contains water, except that the water people seek is living.

See Fellowship as Worship

Jesus defined worship on intersecting planes. He said all the law and the words of the prophets could be summarized in just two statements, "You must love the Lord your God with all your heart, all your soul, and all your mind," and "Love your neighbor as yourself" (Matt. 22:37-39). Your climate of worship should move your people to love each other and God. It should also prod them toward doing good deeds.

Interaction with God through song, liturgy and teaching sets people up with warm feelings and a servant's hearts. Personal interaction with others creates a trailhead toward meaningful ministry. Ministry itself is a form of worship as it gives outlet to spiritual gifts and the love God requires from each person. But for this to happen, you need time and space for your congregation to get to know one another.

Find Time for Fellowship

I had a shocking experience about 10 months into planting our church in Hawaii. A friend of mine visited for the first time. His take was that we were the least-friendly church on Oahu. After dusting off the crumbs of wounded pride, our leadership team reexamined our meetings and practices. We found that we made no provision for people to get to know each other except in our small groups. There was no easy opportunity to build friendships through our worship experience on Sundays. The simple act of providing a three-minute greeting time in the midst of our celebration cracked the ice. Nervous at first, our members soon warmed up to the idea of making friends with the people they sat beside in church. We later helped them along by providing stick-on name badges. We currently stoke the fires of conversation by equipping people with a question to ask and answer during each greeting time.

It is not hard to get God searchers to like each other. But you do have to make a plan and then execute it.

Make a Place for Fellowship

Our church campus looks like a Starbucks café. Green umbrellas preside over patio tables that rest on brick pavement. We serve free snacks and sell other food items. Some of our people treat the location as a second home. It provides an escape from a crowded apartment. More importantly, it is a place to meet others. After meetings people hang around for hours. Throughout the week a person can always find someone to talk with under those umbrellas. Having a place to meet greatly enhances the community aspect of church life, thus supporting our worship experience.

But providing fellowship space can be tough in a portable church. If you rent space for Sunday meetings, then you will need a little innovation. The public school we rented for a decade and a half provided us with lovely alcoves where we could serve food and fellowship with one another out of the sun and rain. One church in our community purchased a half-dozen tentlike portable car covers. Members set them up on the lawn of the local high school each Sunday morning. Another young church adopted a coffee shop as its *place* to go after church and throughout the week for fellowship. A little thought will provide you with an important location to extend the worship experience into the daily life of your congregation.

Create a Unique Style
When our team moved from California to Hawaii, we brought with us a well-developed pattern of worship. We had our own liturgy and a huge repertoire of songs. Within weeks we ditched the whole package. God provided us with local musicians. Some of them wrote their own songs. Their presence tied us to the heart of the community. Their music reflected local tastes. They were familiar faces to many of our first-time attendees. For many of our people, a homegrown worship band compensated for having an outsider in the pulpit.

Music in church should relate to the local culture. Watch a bunch of Baby Boomers sing the original Christian words to the

Drifters' "Stand By Me" and you will understand what I mean. They will shed tears while worshiping God to a song they first heard as love-struck teenagers. Play the U2 spiritual journey song "I Still Haven't Found What I'm Looking For" and you will thrill older Gen-Xers. Build a band that can incorporate local culture into your worship and you will own the loyalty of your community.

> **Helpful Hint:** Incorporate lots of musicians into your program. At Hope Chapel we have different bands for each worship celebration. This builds depth into our overall team and enhances our ability to hand off leadership to new daughter churches. This scheme also gives a musical outlet to more than 100 very talented people. We teach our philosophy of worship to bandleaders. Then we release them to function as they feel the Spirit is leading. The same goes for songwriters. Pray that God brings a songwriter into your mix. Teach that person your philosophy. Then let God use him or her to give a unique voice to your congregation.

Record a Worship CD

It is a good idea to include money for a worship recording session in your first year's budget. Your musicians will love you for it, although they may be less enthusiastic if you hold out for audience participation at the recording session. A group participation album will add fuel to the fires of ownership in a new congregation. A worship CD will extend the range of your church in two other ways. Your people can sing their way to work in the morning as they listen in the car. The album will also double as a calling card for the church when people give it to friends they hope to invite to church.

Worship ties the hearts of God's children to His throne. You have an important task before you, but one that comes with great opportunities and plentiful resources.

CHURCH PLANTER'S CHECKLIST

1. How should worship *feel* in the church you will plant?
2. What style of music would best support this feeling?
3. What percentage of time will you give to worship in each service?
4. What can you do to make worship more interactive than you have ever known it to be?
5. What responses are "legal" in your thinking? Which responses are "illegal"?
6. What can you do to link worship to fellowship?

Note

1. "Westminister Shorter Catechism," *Center for Reformed Theology and Apologetics.* http://www.reformed.org/documents/WSC.html (accessed June 12, 2002).

CHAPTER 15

PREACHING PLAN:
HOW WILL YOU TEACH PEOPLE TO LIVE THEIR FAITH?

A young woman once told me how she was materially blessed by a sermon preached by one of my staff members. She had waited in line for more than 90 minutes to obtain a birth certificate for her newborn baby. As she reached the front of the line, she saw the small sign that read: "Certificate Registration Fee: $10." Carrying a baby but no cash, she broke into tears. At that moment, another woman, who was standing four places behind her, reached forward, handed her a 10-dollar bill and gave her a big smile. She got her certificate, thanked the woman and headed home.

The following Sunday she literally bumped into the same woman outside Hope Chapel. Once the joy had subsided, she asked her new friend why she would give money to a total stranger. The Good Samaritan said she was acting upon a sermon on random acts of kindness she had heard our youth pastor preach two weeks earlier. The moral of this story is that good preaching and teaching pay off in the lives of our members.

YOU NEED A PLAN

It is easy to underestimate the value of teaching and preaching, especially in a church plant. Strategy and organization consume so much of your time and thoughts that you can easily forget that everything you do revolves around the content of your messages. The biblical maxim is true for new churches, too: Faith still comes by hearing and hearing by the Word of God (see Rom. 10:17). Pull yourself away from marketing and logistics long enough to build a preaching plan that will carry you through the first two years. That is a long time, but a new church needs a strong foundation. Rather than be blown by winds of change, you should have a plan in place to fit ideal conditions. That way you will at least know where you stand if circumstances force a change in plans.

Your teaching strategy should set your vision in the context of New Testament life and evangelism, much like a jeweler would center a fine diamond in a setting of golden splendor. There is no universal formula. Every pastor has his or her unique approach. My two-year preaching plan for a new church is very simple. I teach through Philippians, Acts, Romans and 1 Corinthians, in that order.

I use Philippians to ease into congregation life with an upbeat message. This is crowd-gathering time. I use those first few weeks for everyone to get acquainted with our leadership, vision and values. The teaching at that point aims to build a healthy attitude at the formative stage of congregational life.

Acts gives me a pattern for worship and teaching systems. It also teaches how the Early Church approached civil government and evangelism. Working our way through Acts also builds world vision. We finish Acts about six months into church life because I consolidate Paul's last two missionary journeys into one message. I also combine his trips to Jerusalem and Rome.

I then move into Paul's letter to the Romans. The book of Romans forms a theological foundation for the fledgling group. I take roughly 20 weeks to move through Romans. At this point many people leap forward in growth as they come to fully understand God's grace and how it works. As we finish Romans, we learn responsibility toward spiritual gifts and the Body of Christ. We also learn how to dwell together in love.

Helpful Hint: Your message should be positive. Stay upbeat and do not crusade against specific sins or social ills. Preaching through books of the Bible will limit your ability to beat certain subjects to death. It will keep you from riding spiritual hobbyhorses that move people but do not take them anywhere.

First Corinthians deals with love and power. Moving into this book right around our first anniversary allows me to speak into the lives of those people who are beginning to build political positions within our church. We learn to come together around Jesus rather than around individual leaders. Having built a base for love through the last few weeks in Romans and the first few in 1 Corinthians, we are ready to take on the power gifts in the last few chapters of 1 Corinthians.

This plan fits our vision and purpose. It contextualizes our goals in the words and doctrine of the apostles. It moves us beyond a business plan into the realm of the Holy Spirit and His leadership.

CONSIDER WHAT YOU SAY

The content of your teaching matters. I preach from the Bible rather than a manuscript. I publish my notes in the bulletin and project an illustrated version. As a congregation we study the words of Scripture together *in our Bibles* rather than project them on the big screen. This is because I want people to get used to *handling* the Word of God. I repeatedly ask them to write in their Bibles as I teach. I would much rather have them mark their Bible to make it a useful tool than to take copious notes on what I have to say.

We at Hope Chapel sometimes take a little heat for our bibliocentric approach. One time a delegation from another congregation visited my church. As soon as I asked people to open their Bibles to the text for the evening, these people began rolling their eyes and punching each other in the ribs. Later I discovered that they were young pastors in training. They had been taught that it is not sensitive to the unchurched to use the Bible in church. The odd thing about that experience was their reaction as we delved into Scripture. I could see that they were unfamiliar with the content and background of the text. They began the evening as unctuous cynics. They ended it as hungry students.

Let Life Drive Your Teaching

Do not espouse political causes; rather, engage life—including politics—from a biblical perspective. The same advice applies to your approach to current events. Do not let them drive you, but do address them from the pulpit.

I recommend that you read a couple of news magazines each week and be ready to comment on current events within the context of your teaching. However, you should not allow those events to break your stride. The week those jets slammed into the World Trade Center and the Pentagon I was just beginning a series on the life of Joseph. Instead of dropping or interrupting the series, I incorporated the tragic event and its aftermath into my teaching. We learned that what was meant for evil, God can use for good is as true a maxim for modern America as it was for ancient Egypt. My teaching addressed the issue without surrendering to it. Other pastors I know jettisoned their preaching plan to devote their entire effort to the evil events. Some of them ended up creating hysteria rather than calm. Several weeks later, I taught a series on last days Bible prophecy. I used the events of the day against the backdrop of Daniel, Revelation and other texts. Calm prevailed, and I continued to lead my congregation rather than surrender our agenda to those people who created the news.

Learn Your History Lessons

It is wise and often useful if you master and teach history. Your people helplessly flail along without an understanding of the past. Most of them never really learned it in school. Our American educational system has twisted and redefined history with politically correct views. Whenever truth slips into the classroom, it is often suffocated by pillows of peer pressure that knock down any honest attempt to study the lives of dead white men.

My adult son and I once walked Freedom Trail in Boston, Massachusetts. He ate up the historical sites and later commented, "Dad, this is all the stuff that I worked so hard *not* to learn in high school and college. I would study just hard enough to take the tests and then forget everything the minute I walked out of the classroom. We all did—it just wasn't cool to learn history." He went on to describe how the tour made him realize the poverty of his position. Upon returning home, he went on a reading binge. His story is an exception. Unfortunately, you will have to do most of the reading for the busy people in your congregation. View yourself as a designated reader until your teaching entices them to learn on their own. This is part of your readiness to give an answer to those who would ask you for a reason for the hope that lies in your heart.

Do Not Preach Foolishness

It is easy to tell someone, "Don't preach foolishness." To actually do it is harder, since every position you take will look good and wise to you. How do you know whether you are being foolish or standing courageously against the crowd? You can best answer that question by reexamining your position in relationship to your current and historical peers. If your contemporary peer group espouses opinions that vary from the New Testament fathers and from the explosive leaders in Church history, side with the Church fathers. If you find yourself alone in regard to both your current and your historical peers, then you had better take a long, hard look at your ideas. You may be preaching foolishness.

> **Helpful Hint:** Promise yourself that you will never present published sermon illustrations as though they were your own stories—that would be lying. And you know what happens to liars.

While innovation is to be desired, you should avoid goofiness. Your position must be rooted in the Word *and* in the current or past practice of the Church.

Support Your Preaching with Action

Tell stories. Preaching minus application equals boredom. Do not just extract your stories from Internet sites or books of sermon illustrations. Other people's material can be useful, but save them for emergencies. Support your preaching with your own real-life actions. Use the life of your congregation to illustrate your points.

Use your stories to build heroes into the life of your church. Whenever a member does something extraordinary in response to the claims of God's Word, you should brag on them. If someone has unusual insights, tell how they taught you, the teacher. Constantly give examples that support the purpose and mission of the church.

Put a Positive Twist on Negative Stories

Find a way to make a bad situation good. A tradesman in my church in Hawaii told me how he had fallen into sexual sin. He confessed that his fear of losing his girlfriend put him into a situation of great temptation. When she suffered a financial reversal, he invited her to sleep on the couch of his apartment rather than move to another island. They soon slipped and made the mistake. She became pregnant and later lost the baby. His sorrow over the loss of the child was real and intense. His sorrow over the personal failure was even greater. Importantly, he showed great insight when he related the situation to the earlier decision he made to share the apartment. He said, "I fell because I wasn't living my faith. If I had trusted God I would have let her move away and we wouldn't be in this mess." Upon hearing his story, I asked permission to share it with others. I wanted the church to understand that faith translated into works goes beyond doing ministry in church.

At Hope Chapel, we do not talk much about church discipline when it occurs. Rather, whenever it is possible, we link discipline *and* restoration—at the point of restoration. The returning prodigal presents a unique opportunity to show that action has accompanied your message. It also demonstrates that your actions were effective, that "the word of God is full of living power. It is sharper than the sharpest knife, cutting deep into our innermost thoughts and desires" (Heb. 4:12). The testimony of a repentant sinner carries a certain conviction that people living lives of consistent obedience or even of borderline behavior barely understand. When you give a voice to testimonies of restoration, it causes the entire church to engage the Scriptures at a deeper level.

The same standard applies to your own failures and repentance. I recommend that you find ways to work them into your teaching as examples to support your message. A little humorous self-depreciation will help other struggling saints move forward in the Lord. Too many Christians view themselves as the only sinner in a party meant for extremely holy saints. Stories of your personal misadventures in traffic or unnecessary anger toward your spouse will put your people at ease. When they understand that you too are addicted to grace, they will want to try some. Remember you were called to teach God's Word, not to become superman. Your people may want to put you on a spiritual pedestal, but you would be wise to do everyone a favor and refuse to stand on it.

Create Parables That Augment Your Teaching

Follow Jesus' example. He created parables to drive home His messages. You can do the same. Learn to paint word pictures in the imaginations of your listeners. The human imagination delivers glorious action in full and living color. A well-drawn parable will also play lots of reruns in the minds of the hearers. Use the minds and imaginations of your audience to your advantage.

GO BEYOND POWERPOINT

Do not rely on technology. Mention the word "media" to the average American pastor and he will begin talking about how many lumens of light his video projector generates. This is because those projectors are so useful. They are one of the most powerful tools a modern pastor has in his arsenal. Yet, most are underutilized. You can do more with them than simply project words to songs and teaching notes. Sadder yet is the fact that their usefulness tends to overshadow other communications media that is available today. Keep using PowerPoint—probably the most popular medium in churches today—but do not let it limit your thinking and creativity in other areas of communication. Here are a few examples.

Project Testimonials and Drama
At Hope Chapel, we present a testimony or sermon-illustrating drama each week in our celebrations. Testimonies are limited to two minutes. Dramas can extend to four. The testimonies are stories of miraculous answers to prayer, restored families or the blessings that come through small-group fellowship. Each ministry department gets two slots per year, whereas a different small group shows up each month. Drama tends to work better if they are humorous. Amateur writers and actors have a harder time portraying serious emotions. If you choose to use this medium, over time you will develop sophisticated systems for editing and presentation. Do not, however, let the idea that you need to have sophisticated media tools slow you down or scare you away. We started with a rented video camera and no editor. Compensating for our inexperience, we just shot the testimony or drama over and over again until we got it right. Learning as we went along, we soon discovered how this medium captured the imagination of our people. As a bonus, we found that well-presented testimonies made it easy to raise money to buy better equipment.

Include Infomercials on Sunday
At Hope Chapel, we use video productions to present our most important bulletin announcements. The most boring part of

most church meetings is the coming-attractions monologue. We even turned production over to a crew of high school and college students who outdo themselves turning our announcements into award-worthy humor. These video infomercials are often pregnant with truth that reinforces our values and vision. The result is a lot of fun and some additional learning during announcement time. Our people eagerly anticipate announcements in church. Yours will, too.

Employ the Bulletin as a Teaching Tool

A tool as humble as the weekly bulletin offers powerful teaching potential. It is easy to employ it as an extension of your ministry. Simply include a published version of your teaching notes. The notes can carry your teaching into small groups if you choose to use them in that way. Notes published in church bulletins go a long way toward educating and equipping church members. Even if your members do not participate in small groups, they will often use your published notes in their own studies. The notes give structure to their personal examination of God's Word. They also allow your people to transfer the concepts you have taught to their family and friends.

Some people are natural collectors. This type of person will gather your notes into binders. In the process they will further review your teaching. Others will accumulate them in their Bibles only to dispose of them at a later date. Even this modest process creates a teaching opportunity, as many people reread papers before they discard them.

Make a Sermon Series an Event

At one church I visited, the leaders display large posters all over its campus. These compositions can only be compared to the masterpieces found outside movie theatres. Screaming with color, they advertise upcoming events, such as a sermon series or concert. This church wraps its lessons with a wonderful aura of mystique and anticipation. The atmosphere of expectation plows the ground of imagination in the minds of its members. When the ground of people's minds and souls are cultivated, they in turn easily receive seeds of truth.

You might not be financially capable of matching this extreme example, but you can learn from it. Wall space is valuable. A missions conference, baptismal service or guest speaker can be promoted in just a few catchy words that you can fit on a poster. Whatever fills a poster usually works just as well on handbills or flyers. You can have your material printed at a professional shop, or it can be photocopied or printed from a computer. If you rent, you may be forced to post and repost your notices each week, but the opportunities to stimulate your members are still vast.

Banners last longer than handbills. They make great teaching tools. We display our theme for each year on a banner at one side of our auditorium. The other side carries our statement of purpose. I try to refer to one or the other in every teaching session. Use banners to communicate truths you most prefer to instill in the long-term memory of your congregation.

Utilize E-Mail and the Internet
We live in a wonderful era. The apostles would have loved e-mail. They could have touched the ends of Earth without ever leaving Jerusalem.

For very little money you can post each week's message on the Internet in audio form. The ease of access this provides is wonderful for members who may be sitting in hotel rooms when business takes them out of town on a Sunday. Audio postings also allow people who miss a weekend service to participate in small groups built around the message. This form of communication will equip your members to pass your message on to their relatives and friends. If you post the message, accompany it with your printed notes.

Add poster art to your website and you can announce an upcoming series of sermons in advance. Send an e-mail announcement to your congregation, and you will better equip them to invite unchurched people to your fellowship. If someone goes to the trouble to invite their friend to hear a specific message, you can count on them to discuss its truth with that person both before and after your presentation.

Your website also empowers you to network your people to other ministries that focus on apologetics, family helps or specific areas of human need. It is also wise to post any papers you have in your own arsenal that address need-meeting subjects.

UNDERSTAND THE POWER OF RITUAL

One time, when I was officiating at a wedding, I looked up and saw that a hardened politician was in the crowd. His wife openly wept through the ceremony, and at one point I noticed a tear streaming down his cheek. After the wedding, they both went out of their way to tell me how much they appreciated my words. They admitted that their marriage was feeling the wear and tear of public life. They thanked me for helping them repair their feelings toward one another and toward their holy union. For them, the ceremony was a form of marriage therapy.

If you approach weddings as more than ceremonies they can function as opportunities for mass marriage counseling. But weddings are not the only occasion you have to change the thinking of large groups of people, many of whom may be unchurched. Let's consider some of the ritual functions you will certainly include as a church planter. A little innovation can turn these into great prospects for shaping thought and behavior. The question we should ask is, How can we turn often boring events into rich teaching opportunities?

Let Baptisms Become Celebrations

I met Percy Brewster two months before I became a pastor. He was a well-aged warhorse of a man. He had pastored successful churches in England and Wales as far back as the turn of the last century. I asked him what advice he could give a 25-year-old ministry novice who was about to plant his first church. He told me to major in water baptism. Through the years He had observed that public baptism prompted converts to move forward in the Lord. Those who held back from baptism usually fell away. I took his advice and my new church invested heavily in water baptism.

We turned baptisms into large celebrations of God's grace in the lives of new believers. Converts invited their relatives and friends to witness the personal spiritual milestone. We would often hold a picnic after the baptism service. This created an opportunity for our members to befriend any guests. We soon found that baptisms by the beach are more exciting than those held inside a church.

Baptisms, above all else, offer an opportunity to present the gospel to people who need to hear it. You can briefly explain baptism and its relationship to salvation. Then allow the person being baptized to give testimony to the change in his or her life since he or she came into relationship with Jesus Christ. Finally, permit one of his or her friends or relatives to corroborate the changes he or she has observed in the life of the person being baptized. Often a non-Christian will testify to the changes Jesus has made in his or her friend. Many guests at baptisms become Christians in the weeks that follow the baptism. At Hope Chapel, almost all of the non-Christians who have testified eventually found the Lord. They could not escape their own description of the power of the gospel.

Allow Communion to Become Fellowship

Let other members of your staff and congregation lead Communion services. This will give people a break from always hearing your voice. This action insures a fresh approach to Communion each time you celebrate it. Nothing kills enthusiasm as effectively as a dull routine.

Look for a creative way to share the elements. Try to move away from the Protestant ritual of passing cups and crackers down the aisles. At Hope Chapel, we give a brief Communion message then invite the people to move to tables strategically set about the room. People quietly pick up the bread and wine set at the tables, then step aside to pray and share Communion informally in very small groups or family units. We encourage everyone to straighten out any twisted or angry relationships before they take Communion. This follows Paul's lead (see 1 Cor. 11). If you visit our church during Communion, you will see our people weeping in each other's arms during this time of focused worship. For us, Communion is an opportunity to act out love and unity.

Reach the Adults During a Baby Dedication

A baby dedication is a great time to get adults to face the issue of integrity. I have found that it works to bring the extended church family into a commitment toward an innocent child. You can do this as well. Lead the adults in prayer. Have them pledge to live straight-and-true lives in front of the ever-watching child. Ask the parents to dedicate more than the child to the Lord. They can promise to bring their child up in a godly manner and to live a lifestyle that would reflect their faith. At Hope Chapel, we call upon the entire church to admit to their influence on the life of any child in our midst. Every baby we dedicate reminds us of Jesus' words: "If anyone causes one of these little ones . . . to lose faith, it would be better for that person to be thrown into the sea with a large millstone tied around the neck" (Matt. 18:6).

Involve Everyone in Holiday Programs

Christmas, Easter and Mother's Day come laced with opportunities for your church to grow. Let the children put on a special musical or drama presentation—you will experience a bulge in attendance. You will make lots of contacts among all the aunts, uncles and grandparents who will come to see their relative. You can follow up with each one of them. New churches that do not involve children at the holidays tend to shrink because people retreat to whichever church, restaurant or reunion has traditionally tied together their nuclear family. You can help your members create new traditions that center around your church.

How do you capture the attention of the newcomers who come to see the children? Throw meaningful apologetics into an otherwise romantic holiday celebration, or tie warm holiday feelings to history. I especially love Thanksgiving because it provides an opportunity to bridge the Reformation to democracy and the current American way of life. By teaching our spiritual heritage, I welcome others into it. With these added elements of apologetics and history you will engage the minds of people who previously ranked Christianity as anti-intellectual. Some of them may have even given up on God.

When your church offers a stimulating holiday fare, it instills courage in your members. They will be more apt to invite their friends and relatives if they believe the program is rich and worth their time. Some of those who come will become regular holiday attendees. It may take three or four years of holiday visits before they accept Christ into their lives. Others will convert more easily.

Equip Your Leaders Through Commissioning Services

Lay hands on your leaders to ordain them as pastors of small groups. At Hope Chapel, we do this when we send someone out to plant a new church. But we also lay hands on those who step forward to pastor our small groups or MiniChurches. The process brings spiritual and emotional support to the people undertaking the serious task of shepherding part of the flock of God. It also reminds the congregations of our values and goals. We link these commissioning services to our calling to equip every member to take God's love to every person. When we do this, the people in the audience are reminded of their roles in God's kingdom.

When we commission new MiniChurch pastors, we present the person who mentored them with an aluminum baton similar to the ones used in track meets. An inscription on the baton commemorates their successful handing off of their ministry to the person who they discipled. It also celebrates their courage and sacrifice as they step out to plant a new MiniChurch.

Pray at Special Events

When you plant a church, it will not be long before you are invited to pray at community functions. Your people will submit your name in an effort to give you visibility in the community. Their goal is to market your church. That is valid, but you can do much more with the opportunity if you cautiously reach beyond prayer. With a few words of teaching, you will be able to impart values to community leaders.

When it comes to community prayers, boredom is your friend. Public prayers are often quite similar and usually perfunctory. This works in your favor. Before praying speak about some issue facing the community, but do not take more than a minute. Then pray for that problem. You will have the attention of every person in that audience.

At one public function I voiced our church's absolute support for public school administrators and then suggested that the schools would be a better place if all teachers were required to enroll their children rather than send them to private schools. I held the audience's attention when I went on to pray for the schools to solve the union-versus-management crisis they faced.

On another occasion, hecklers showed up to embarrass our governor at the groundbreaking ceremony of a school gymnasium. Before I prayed, I spoke publicly to the governor, pointing out a bunch of high school kids who had erected a banner in his support. I told him that although I did not vote for him, I supported him as my leader and appreciated his efforts to better our schools, as did that handful of students. I then prayed for unity in our community.

At our mayor's inauguration, I mentioned the economic crisis that faced our city. I spoke of God's desire to bless people who turn to Him for help. Then, just like everyone before me at every inaugural since the founding of the city, I said a prayer for divine guidance. However, my opening words caused those present to mentally process the prayer rather than turn it off as religious mumbo-jumbo.

In each of these situations I received personal expressions of gratitude from non-Christian members of the audience. They appreciated the idea of a church shaping values in the community. I cannot say that these events bring many people into church. The marketing value *is* limited. However, they are opportunities to be the salt of the earth.

CHURCH PLANTER'S CHECKLIST

1. Try to sketch, in broad strokes, a two-year teaching plan. Then schedule a three-day prayer retreat where you will fill in the details down to the topic and Scriptures references.

2. Write three paragraphs that describe your style as a preacher and teacher. Now write two more to suggest how you could make your teaching more interactive.

3. What could you do to make the following opportunities richer preaching experiences?

   • Baptism
   • Communion
   • Baby dedications
   • Easter
   • Thanksgiving
   • Christmas

CHAPTER 16

MONEY:
HOW CAN YOU ENJOY STRONG STEWARDSHIP?

Money problems can cripple a new church. If you have too little it restricts ministry. If you have too much it tends to limit your dependence on the Holy Spirit. Finding balance is a ticklish trick. It requires that you build financial responsibility into the new congregation, starting the first week.

POINT YOUR PEOPLE TOWARD STEWARDSHIP

We moved to Hawaii with very strong backing from the church I left in California. It would have been easy to succumb to financial comfort. We counteracted complacency by giving away our entire offering the first Sunday. We met in a park at the beach with no immediate prospect of indoor meeting space that would require rent. We could not fully project our financial needs, yet we gave our entire offering to another Hope Chapel that was planted that same morning in Salt Lake City, Utah. Our rationale was that they faced a more difficult mission field than we did. Our goal was to teach our people faith and the responsibility of stewardship. We wanted them to know that we trusted God to bless us if we gave. We also wanted to build our church on a foundation of responsibility to the task of building the kingdom of God.

Look for Outside Financial Support

Unless you start a house church, you will need help from beyond your new congregation. As I have already noted, this support should come from a parent church, denominational resources and generous friends. Paul commended the poor Philippians for their generosity while he chided the rich Corinthians for failure to follow through with their gifts. He taught that generous giving results in equality of resources and the blessing of God (see 2 Cor. 8:1-15). But financial stewardship must eventually be a product of your own healthy congregation. At some point you must move from a position of accepting resources to one of generously giving them. Your financial health will eventually reflect your teaching on the subject.

End Outside Funding Early

External financial aid is in itself a powerful teaching device, but the results will depend upon how you manage it. Prolonged support can teach a congregation an unhealthy dependence on human resources. Overdependence tends to generate anger toward generous sponsors. Dependency causes recipients to think they should get more than they do. This is because it dulls their sense of personal responsibility; it even causes them to do little with the gifts they receive. The antidote to this illness can be found in early cessation of funding.

When you relinquish funds before they are due to expire, you create a pride and independence in your young congregation. You also teach that God is the only dependable source of blessing. Announce your intentions to terminate support early in the process. Use the announcement to embrace financial independence as a core value in your new church. Along with this announcement you should teach your people that the church needs their consistent support.

Personal independence commingled with spiritual dependence breeds health in any church. Abraham displayed these attitudes when he refused the bounty offered to him by the king of Sodom. He declined the king's gifts and stated, "I have solemnly promised the LORD, God Most High, Creator of heaven and earth, that I will not take so much as a single thread or sandal thong from you. Otherwise you might say, 'I am the one who made Abram rich!'" (Gen. 14:22-23).

Give While Receiving
The Philippians gave out of their poverty (see 2 Cor. 8:2). Paul praised them for doing so. He also promised them that God "will supply all your needs from his glorious riches, which have been given to us in Christ Jesus" (Phil. 4:19). What was true in ancient Philippi is also valid in your city. God endows generous people with His bounty.

Become a generous source of funds for others while you operate under outside support. Let your corporate actions teach your people stewardship and generosity. In my first church, we gave large gifts to missionaries and poverty-stricken people even while my family was living off of personal savings. The people who knew the condition of our finances were amazed that we could trust the Lord during such difficult circumstances. Many increased their own giving as a result. They became foundational leaders and examples to the rest of the congregation. Generosity begets generosity. But you have to act out the message for it to grip people's hearts.

Never Beg for Money

Televangelists and radio preachers who plead for money turn off people everywhere. Those media ministers make your job much harder. Their unwarranted excess creates a negative stereotype and forces you to diligently display integrity when you talk about money.

I remember attending large Christian youth rallies when I was a high school student. The leaders would sneak up on the offering. They worked very hard to cover their tracks, but the appeal always came down to the same sentiment: "We desperately need your money and you should sacrifice tonight's hamburger and Coke for this ministry—or we will go out of business." My friends and I grew so cynical that we stopped giving altogether. We made a game out of it. We would try to discern changes in the onstage production, and we would guess when they would actually begin the offering presentation. After we timed the offering, we developed ratios that compared the overall number of minutes in the service to the amount of time devoted to the offering. When a preacher begged for money, it had a reverse effect on us. We were not so unique. If you plead for larger offerings, you will see your members react the same way, and your church's income will not increase.

Be Positive About Money

Always assume that God is in control—because He is. Communicate confidence to your people. From that base of assurance you can present the needs and goals of the church.

You should help your people see that they too are responsible for the vision and expenses of the church. Do this by letting them know the true financial picture. Painting a clear financial picture does not require hysterics. You can and would be wise to open your books and your heart. However, repel the temptation to press the panic button when the news is bad. Even when you have serious needs, maintain an even temper and show your people that you trust in God, not your own ability to raise money.

It is wise to keep complainers in line and to keep them from stealing your agenda. There will always be people who feel it is "unspiritual" to talk about money in church. Jesus condemned those who brag about their financial gifts. Yet in the Gospels, we see that He repeatedly spoke about money.

Talk about money, but do it in an open, honest and positive manner. My experience has shown me that this approach will start people in the right direction toward proper stewardship.

Have Fun Building Your Budget
Your budget should directly reflect your vision and purpose. Planning should quantify steps toward your announced mission. Those steps should tie directly to dates on a calendar. A budget is merely price tags attached to a calendar of plans. If the calendared expenses tally higher than projected income, you have decisions to make. You can cut back on scheduled actions, or you can raise more money. If you draw your people into the planning process, they are more likely to choose the second alternative. Let a broad-based group of people author the budget. If they have been involved in the strategizing, then they will be more excited about paying the bills.

At Hope Chapel, we maintain E-teams (E stands for excellence). These are leadership units that serve every one of our ministries. Each year we assemble all of our E-team members for several hours of mutual planning. As senior pastor, I outline the theme and overall mission objectives for the coming year. We then break the event into several planning segments built around those objectives.

Each group assembles a set of goals pertaining to their separate ministry. They build their goals into a calendar of events. An "event" might be anything from an outreach to a music presentation to the purchase of a piece of equipment. After the meeting the staff contact for that E-team meets with the entire ministry team to attach costs to the events. Each staff member then contributes his or her gathered costs to the main budget. Of course, the budget must meet overall priority requirements and gets revised several times until projected costs fit with projected income. The planning process stretches over three months. It is fun for the several hundred people who participate in it. They know they have a say in the operation of their church. They also feel committed to do whatever it takes to make their ministry dreams come true. Involved planners are motivated givers.

Teach Tithing

Pastors need to teach their people to give—more specifically, to tithe.

The concept of tithing comes under fire from some quarters of the Christian Church. Attackers say that the tithe is a principle taught in the Law of Moses and not applicable to Christians living under grace. Tithing, like marriage, is biblical. Similar to marriage it was introduced before the imposition of the Mosaic law (see Gen. 14:20; 28:22). The law embraces the concept, as it does the institution of marriage. Jesus endorsed tithing, as He did marriage. At least one other New Testament writer underscored tithing in the book of Hebrews. To marginalize the concept in some way is to marginalize your thinking. To do so also removes some wonderful promises regarding financial blessing.

God promises to give back to us according to what we invest in His kingdom: "If you give, you will receive. Your gift will return to you in full measure, pressed down, shaken together to make room for more, and running over. Whatever measure you use in giving—large or small—it will be used to measure what is given back to you" (Luke 6:38). The idea of a measure in giving is important because your people will want some sort of guiding principle to associate with their giving. The only such principle suggested in Scripture is the tithe.

The principle comes with a purpose and a promise. Malachi told God's people the tithe was to ensure that there would be food in the storehouse. His words directly relate the tithe to the physical needs and resources of a church. His instruction will make sense to your people: *ministry costs money*.

He further promised a blessing upon the families of those who tithe: "I will open the windows of heaven for you. I will pour out a blessing so great you won't have enough room to take it in! Try it! Let me prove it to you!" (Mal. 3:10). The promise ties the hope of material prosperity to an offer to test God at His word. This is the only place in Scripture where the Lord invites us to test His promise. I find the idea of a test instructional to people who are skeptical about the connection between money and Church. I always present this challenge: "Try tithing for three months. If you experience noticeable blessing during that time, keep tithing. If you don't see God's blessing—quit tithing." It is a pretty simple proposition. Your people need the blessings God promises. Your church needs food in the storehouse.

Make a Schedule

Redundancy can be a good teacher. If you want your people to embrace a particular truth or remember the Red Sea miracle stories of how your church came to be, tell them often. I strongly suggest that you take at least two weeks to deal with primary subjects and issues, but the amount of time spent will depend upon the topic and your circumstances. Some requisites for any church include "How to Have a Healthy Marriage," "How to Serve Christ Through His Church" and "How to Be a Good Financial Steward."

If you want your members to understand tithing and become tithers, go over the principles again and again. Schedule a time to teach about giving and tithing—I suggest at least once a year. At Hope Chapel, I try to preach for at least two consecutive weeks on tithing each spring, right after people pay their income taxes. I have taught on the subject for as many as four weekends in a row. Sometimes the message comes within the context of a longer series about overall financial stewardship. On other occasions, I simply address Scriptures that deal with tithing. In addition to the designated sermons, throughout the year I use illustrations of how God has blessed my own finances and the finances of others in our church. I also try to focus on giving and tithing in messages and special offerings in the fall and during the Christmas season.

There was a time when I was paranoid about preaching on tithes. I feared that the first-timer might be turned off by the message. However, experience has taught me that the only people who become angry over sermons on tithing are Christians who resist learning the biblical lesson. Newcomers usually thrill over the strong promises of financial freedom offered in Scripture. Furthermore, in an ironic twist, I have found that tithing messages are often followed by larger than usual numbers of people praying to receive Christ.

I also fear that when I preach on tithing I will bore the long-time members of my church. Tithing sermons tend to focus on the same set of Scriptures year after year. But I have discovered that faithful tithers love to hear the message. They have seen God's blessings and want others to be blessed as well. I am so convinced of this that I send prayer letters to the most faithful givers in our database, announcing when I will deliver my messages on tithing. These people provide me with extra prayer support as those weekends approach. Anticipating my every word, they become cheerleaders rather than students.

Tap Various Teaching Tools

Do not try to be the only voice on this subject. I enlist the most dedicated tithers to teach others. Some of our strongest tithing messages have come from laypeople. They present these truths in clearer, more practical terms than I do. They speak with great conviction that rises out of the results they have seen in their own lives. They also do not have to deal with the obvious conflict of interest that I do. Their salaries do not come out of our tithes.

At Hope Chapel, we host a couple of financial-management seminars each year, specifically for people with histories of spending problems. Laypeople skilled in financial matters run these seminars. They also offer private counseling after the training. We maintain a library of audiocassettes, brochures and other tools to support this important area of Christian life. As a follow-up on these seminars, we often let people share their testimonies when they get their financial lives together. Most of the testimonies we hear center on the blessings that come from putting the tithing concept into practice.

Report Results to Your People

No one wants to spend a lifetime pumping water out of a sinking ship. If your financial discussions always center on *need,* your people will lose confidence in your ministry. Report *results,* and you will instill hope and enthusiasm in your congregation.

You can fall into the trap of only discussing money when you are short of it. You would do better to restrict your discussions to the good things that result from the current level of giving. Reporting is easy: Just compare your actual income to your budget. Your people will appreciate it if you post it in your weekly bulletin. You should report both contemporaneous and year-to-date figures. When you take a special offering, always report the results and compare them to the target figure. Compliment your congregation when you do well. Your kind words will keep them focused on the financial needs of the church. Report special projects and missionary results by way of testimonies and illustrations within your sermons. Always keep your people informed of the financial health of their church. Marry your financial results to your vision. Remind them that the budget is only the financial expression of this year's attempt to fulfill your mission. Help them see that the expenses are the result of your church family doing good things in people's lives, in your community and around the world.

Elevate the Church Board as a Financial Pillar
Select people from the pool of apparent tithers who will stand for election or appointment (depending upon your governmental philosophy) to your church board. It is not wise to allow someone to oversee the spending of your church's finances if he or she is not a systematic giver.

Your board should not make day-to-day financial decisions; rather, they are there to ensure that you make good ones. Their job is to hold you accountable to your own vision and goals as the primary leader in the congregation. A very serious part of their job is that of helping you maintain financial accountability and integrity. Mention their role during church elections (if you have them) and every other time you can wedge it in. Teach your people that they can trust your leadership because you are accountable to the board.

Put Strong Givers on Your Prayer Team

When you need to report bad news, take it to your strongest givers first. They will be most invested in the financial life of the church, so you can trust them to stand with you in prayer. I maintain a personal prayer team of people living in various parts of the world. But when faced with financial crisis, I go to a smaller team composed of givers at the local level. This keeps our bad news much more private than if we broadcast it to the larger prayer list. It also gives me an opportunity to vent my fears and frustrations to people with whom I interact on a daily basis. I crave their support.

Sometimes your prayer letter to givers will reap extra giving on their part, but that should not be the primary purpose for this kind of communiqué. At times, people on your list will respond to your letter with wise advice that fills a knowledge gap in your toolbox. You will benefit from their insight. But the priority of these letters is prayer.

The ability to gather prayer support from committed people during times of financial crisis will keep you from crying wolf in public. The prayers will also garner results. There is strength in numbers: "I also tell you this: If two of you agree down here on earth concerning anything you ask, my Father in heaven will do it for you. For where two or three gather together because they are mine, I am there among them" (Matt. 18:19-20).

CHURCH PLANTER'S CHECKLIST

1. What could you do in your first month to invest a spirit of generosity in your new church?
2. What dangers can you identify in your financial support system as it stands today?
3. Design the budget process you will use when your church is one year old. How can you involve a broad range of people in this process?
4. Do you believe that the Scriptures teach the principle of tithing in the twenty-first century? How will your belief translate into generous giving in your church?
5. List five communication tools that you might develop to keep your members informed about your church's financial situation.

CHAPTER 17

MEMBERSHIP:
HOW CAN YOU LEVERAGE YOUR VISION AS A LEADERSHIP TOOL?

When my wife and I planted the church in Hawaii, people kept asking us when we thought we would return to the mainland. They viewed our committment to them as temporary. As a result, they were slow to invest their trust in us or in the church. We continued to face this question until the moment we bought a house. After the close of escrow, we never heard the question again. Our new friends found the reassurance they sought. They now felt confident that the relationships we built would last over time. They did not want to join a *system* called "church," but they would align with a spiritual family they could call their own.

Church membership seems inconsequential to most post-modern people. This is because it is couched in terms of corporations and systems. While institutional membership may mean little to members of the younger generations, making some kind of commitment remains valuable. This is an important biblical concept. Jesus stood against the institutionalization of the Pharisees. Yet He taught the principle of personal commitment from a point of integrity. Paul considered commitment a family issue so important that he compared church members to parts of a human body. Cut them off, he wrote, and they cannot survive (see Rom. 12:4-5). Integrity of membership breathes life into any church that handles it in a positive manner. You will reap great benefits if you burn a biblical concept of membership into the hearts of your people.

OFFER A KIND OF MEMBERSHIP POSTMODERNS WILL ACCEPT

I am a Baby Boomer. We are the first postmodern generation. Mine is the generation that rejects tradition, labeling it inauthentic and plastic. The leftists among us regard religion as an opiate useful only to tame the masses. All through our sexual revolution we discarded the stability of marriage for the pleasures of casual relationships. We delegated many of our parental responsibilities to nursery schools and the public education system. As we have begun to reach maturity, however, we are rediscovering the need for many of the values and institutions that we once abandoned. Gen-Xers and Millennials grew up in the social vacuum we created. Today's world cries out for legitimacy in government, religion, family and tradition. If joining a church is like joining a club, postmoderns will not stomach it. They will see it as fraudulent. However, if church

membership approximates immersion into a large family, it becomes attractive.

Postmoderns crave authenticity.[1] This involves committed
relationships. Gen-Xers often find more security with a self-
selected family of close friends than they did in the one that
gave them birth. As a result, Gen-Xers intensely parent and
protect their own children. Growing up without fathers has
left many Gen-Xers and Millennials hungry for mentors. Any
adult willing to invest his or her life in a postmodern person
can engender a healthy legacy of love and learning. Young
adults are idealistic and want to improve the world as they pass
through. This tendency makes them willing to make sacrifices
for well-defined causes. They will build their lives around a
clearly stated mission. Millennials in particular seem set to
invest their lives in the extension of causes, including the right
church.

I became a pastor during a time of social chaos. My peers
questioned and tried to overthrow the establishment. As a
young pastor, I brought my doubts into the ministry. I saw
church membership as a meaningless detail. To me it was just
another tool for control in the hands of the religious bureaucra-
cy. For years we treated formal membership with the lightest
possible touch. Our membership book contained names, but no
words of commitment or creeds. You joined the family by simply
pooling your name with the others. In other words, we asked
nothing of our members. There were even some new churches in
that era that did not even enroll members.

Looking back, I still think church membership *had* degener-
ated into the nonsense we perceived it to be. But our response to
its sad state was just as silly. Meaningful membership was always
right before us in the form of the apostle's teaching throughout
the New Testament. A return to New Testament values is the
only solution to confusion about valid church membership.

At Hope Chapel we view membership in the church like membership in our own families. There is a commitment to participate in all the fellowship and joy. There is also an unspoken demand to participate in the chores and costs. Beyond that there is a loyalty to the family that comes from belonging to one another. Much of this can be quantified and tied to a membership covenant, as we do in our basic commitments (I cover this later in this chapter). However, the essence of membership is somewhat mystical and still relates to Jesus having placed us in a particular congregation because we fit with its people.

Do Not Major in Doctrine and Denomination

Postmodern people are often labeled as "post-denominational" because they care little about large-scale affiliations. Their loyalties are directed toward people they can know on a personal level, not institutions. Your church's membership covenant should reflect this trend. Do not complicate it with doctrinal statements. You need them, but the membership contract is not the place to specify them. Do not tie local church membership to a relationship with an impersonal denomination and its leaders whom the prospective member has never met or heard of. Instead, you should focus on immediate relationships reflected in Jesus' commands to love the Lord and our neighbors.

Take Advantage of Strong Metaphors

Our apostolic fathers used visual and poetic metaphors to describe healthy relationships among Christians. They said nothing about pledges or membership books, which should never be confused with the Book of Life. Every description they left for us is relational. The bonding agent is always our common friendship with the Lord. The Church is to be a body and Christ is to be the head (see Eph. 4:15-16). View the church as a temple and Christ as the builder *and* the chief cornerstone (see 1 Pet. 2:4-5). When the church understands this and then sees itself as a family, it centers on Christ as the patriarch (see Eph. 2:19-20).

Members of this unit we call Church are called into mutual service. Spiritual gifts equip each person who is in Christ's Body to serve the other members—there is a calling or assignment associated with membership (see Rom. 12:3-13). The New Testament extends no appeal to organizational strength or allegiances. Instead, it declares that love *binds* the members of God's family to one another. It underlies the roadbed for sacrifice to the worldwide cause of the gospel (see 1 Cor. 13:3). As salt and light, members lose themselves in a value system that redefines everything, including their own identity (see Matt. 5:13-14).

Helpful Hint: When people align themselves with your church, they will want to know where you have come from, why you are there and where you plan to take them. It is your task to show them how God can satisfy their desire for a purpose in life and how belonging to your church can help bring that purpose to life.

I have included only a handful of New Testament metaphors for the church. As you search your Bible, you will find many others. They glue us together with our forebears and with each other in the family of God. Each is a powerful motivator. They are alive and powerful words capable of cutting between our soul and spirit. A teaching series looking at just the few that I included on these pages could set the tone for authentic membership in your new church. Knowledge of these truths will enable your people to commit themselves to each other and to anchor themselves to God.

Link Your Vision and Your Members

Everyone needs a cause. When we subscribe to a cause that is larger than our own lives, it gives us a reason to life. The Bible addresses this need: "Where there is no vision, the people perish" (Prov. 29:18, *KJV*).

The task will not be an easy one. Most people will want to fill that emptiness inside with services you provide *for* them. Yet they will not be truly satisfied until they learn to *serve others*.

In Paul's last meeting with the Ephesian elders, he summarized his own life with Jesus' words: "It is more blessed to give than to receive" (Acts 20:35). Paul's admonition was for those leaders to walk with his dedication to the gospel. He described a life that found meaning in *sacrifice*. Jesus' words are as true for those people who will discover Christ through your church as they were for Paul or the Ephesian Christians.

True contentment comes from sacrifice. Sacrifice for a cause satisfies more deeply than even the random acts of kindness they perform. Your people need your vision in order to complete their Christian experience.

Vision, purpose and mission must occupy much of the agenda at a gathering for prospective members. Flying the flag of vision will ignite the flames of excitement in the hearts of even novice Christians. But commonality of vision will do more than energize people—it will bring form and substance to every endeavor of your church.

Let Your Vision Set the Boundaries

A clearly stated vision can set boundaries for church activities. If members understand what it is that you are trying to accomplish, they will also know what you *do not* intend to pursue. A clear-cut understanding will prevent false starts toward off-focus ministry pursuits. I know pastors who never state their vision. Then they spend their days in anger toward people who do not support it. These pastors become angriest with those whom they perceive as rebellious toward their missions. These rebellious mishaps would never occur if they established a common understanding from the outset. Promote your vision at membership meetings and welcome events. Be sure everyone knows what they are getting into.

A clearly stated vision is important because it is so easy to get sidetracked. In Hawaii, we could have had conflict with one of our most devoted workers because of poorly defined boundaries. This woman started a great ministry discipling people with special needs in small groups. From there she naturally got involved in their social needs—so far so good. But then she built a project designed to provide school supplies for poor children who live in Waikiki—about 20 miles from our church. This last project, while well intended, had nothing to do with discipleship or equipping people for ministry. Although she had invested much time and energy in the project, she quickly adjusted when we put on the brakes. Another person might not have been as flexible. My point is that that the fault here was truly my own. Had I better specified boundaries to our vision she would not have pursued the venture.

Set Boundaries and Grant Permission for Creative Ministry
While an unambiguous vision establishes boundaries, it also licenses creativity. Your church will grow faster if you establish an atmosphere of permission. If people see needs, they should be able to fill them without asking for permission. Approval should be implied within the boundaries of vision.

I once saw a bumper sticker that said "Think globally, act locally." That sentiment ought to be true in your church. Your people should think in terms of your corporate vision. Then they should be able to act individually when they encounter a need or opportunity. What I call autonomy-in-concert can accomplish great things.

General permission motivates individuals. But it supplies even stronger medicine for groups of dedicated volunteers. Your ministry teams should know that they are free to pursue goals as they see them. Innovation thrives only on the fresh air of permission. Creative people will instigate ideas far beyond your dreams—if you grant them permission within bounds.

When I was in junior high school, my parents defined my turf. I could ride my bicycle anywhere within an area of quiet streets bounded by four heavily traveled highways. I was never to cross the busy roads. I also had to be home by a certain time each afternoon. They gave me two hours of freedom within a domain of one square mile. I managed to get into a little trouble and occasionally strayed across those boundaries, but life worked better for me and for them because I understood that I had permission to act within bounds and I understood the bounds. The same will be true for your people if you use your vision to license freedom within its parameters.

Helpful Hint: When someone steps out of bounds, define his behavior as exactly that. Do not impute any other motive than an honest attempt to serve God and your church. Tell him or her clearly where and why the invention does not fit the parameters of your vision. End by thanking him or her for his or her willingness to serve and by telling him or her that you need his or her continued passion for ministry. If possible, redirect his or her efforts into an area that better fits with your vision. In the process, never back down from your role as the primary vision caster for the church. But be willing for God to stretch your boundaries through the person who has stepped across the line. Together you might become very inventive.

Allow Your Vision to Work as a Peacekeeper
New members eventually lead ministry teams and church boards. An early infusion of vision will establish and later provide commonality of understanding at leadership levels. Much

of the tension between pastors and church boards has roots in a lack of agreed-upon vision and values. In successful churches, board members come and go. Pastors remain in place for long periods of time. Many unsuccessful churches see the inverse of this scenario. Board members repeat their terms incessantly while pastoral turnover is alarmingly high. In all churches, the pastor functions much like a CEO does in a corporation. He is the provider and keeper of vision. As pastor, it will be your job to so infuse new people with vision that they always live under its cover—especially when they ascend to your board. Most board-room arguments will die when held up to a church's vision or purpose statements. Solutions glow suddenly obvious in the light of commonly held beliefs.

Measure New Projects Against Your Vision

Well-stated vision offers a realistic measuring device for involvement with new projects. It also provides a tool to gauge the success of ongoing ministries. You can use your vision to filter whether or not to invest church resources in the passions and promises of an individual. If a scheme is closely aligned with your vision, you invest heavily. If a plan marginally overlaps with your vision, then you can decide to offer only marginal support so that you remain focused on your primary goals.

Real power comes when you measure ongoing ministry functions. Goals must reflect the priorities inherent in your vision and mission statements. Goals you achieve will function as a reward for sacrifice. Unmet targets will call for reprioritization of time and other resources. Set long-range objectives to guide you as you establish shorter-term goals. Frame your long-term objectives in line with decades. Doing so will create a framework for annual planning. Long-term objectives are easier to link to vision and mission statements. Short-term goals and success measurements should emerge from your longer projections.

As I have already noted, you will better communicate your vision and people will be more apt to stay in line with it if you publish it. Write it down in some form, perhaps as a formal statement, and make it available.

DEFINE HEALTH MEMBERSHIP WITH THESE FIVE COMMITMENTS

Here are the five questions we ask every potential new member at Hope Chapel. They *make up* our membership covenant. All of them reflect an immediate relationship with our local congregation and its people. They define the costs of membership.

Do You Love Jesus Christ and Acknowledge Him as the Lord of Your Life and All Creation?

We want people to join our church for only one major reason: to grow closer to God. We are aware of valid secondary motives. Some come hoping to find a marriage partner. Others come because their family is in trouble. Many come because of loneliness. Most want to make the world a better place. All are valid reasons. But our top priority is to sharply focus on the one relationship that validates all the others.

Do You Respect Your Church Leaders and Their Vision?

The second relational issue is the prospective member's attitude toward established leadership. I do not believe a person should join a congregation if he or she feels unsure about the leadership. I actually ask people if they *like* our leadership team. It is pretty hard to enjoy serving the Lord if you have to follow someone you do not like. Acting out a vision you do not believe in is impossible. We want people to join our church only if they feel a sense that the Holy Spirit has assigned them to our leadership team. By its very nature, that assignment must coincide with the vision and mission of the church.

Along these lines, we ask people if they are comfortable with the way we have organized our congregation. In our church family, a person will counsel with lay leaders rather than professional pastors. We prevail upon our members to participate in small groups. They will feel peer pressure moving them toward active ministry. Everything we do reflects our desire for everyone to be very active in the church. At times we are messy and eclectic because of our strong reliance on volunteers. That messiness is woven into the fabric of the church. We will not sacrifice excellence, but we do reserve the right to train some people as they learn—accepting their mistakes along the way. We always have lots of newcomers learning on the job. Anyone seeking to join must feel safe in this environment. Our church favors the rising generation. This means our music style is always in flux. It also means that current, sometimes radical, styles of dress will find their way into our midst. Our leaders will always err toward grace if someone appears out of place or out of step.

All this requires grace in the hearts of prospective members. A person who feels uncomfortable with our style and organization is actually frustrated by our leadership team. To move forward with such a relationship can only hurt everyone involved. We try to counsel such people to find another church. The goal is mutual satisfaction rather than friction between leaders and members.

Are You Willing to Spend Time with the Church Family?

We want our members to love each other. Love requires partnership, which is a product of time spent together. Every church offers a rich community to those who fully participate. Yet, Christianity is an isolated exercise for too many people. They attend services with people they do not know. Then, at the close of the meeting, they all too quickly rush to the exits. From the Day of Pentecost onward, as is shown in the New Testament, friendship was—and still is—koinonia, or partnering together (see Acts 2:42). This close-knit fellowship suggests a commitment to ownership of the church. Ownership at this level only occurs when people take time for each other.

People who spend time with each other come to a better appreciation of each other, the church and our mutual mission. At Hope Chapel, we encourage every person who attends our services to cultivate at least one solid and serious friendship with another member. More than 85 percent of our people came to the church because a friend invited them. This means that most of our attendees already have at least one contact in our congregation. Our job is to make sure they slow down enough to enjoy that friendship to its fullest benefit. Anyone joining one of our small groups or ministry teams will immediately understand the results of partnership in our church. The love we share in those groups and teams conveys the power of God to individual lives. Koinonia produces spiritual results never found by merely attending church services.

The Bible prods us to "consider how we may spur one another on toward love and good deeds" (Heb. 10:24, *NIV*). It also teaches us how we can do that: "Let us not give up meeting together" (Heb. 10:25, *NIV*). Sunday meetings are great times for training and for worship. However, the small group is where people encourage one another in an exchange of love and friendship. At Hope Chapel, we teach our people that membership is impossible if they cannot or will not invest a couple of hours per week in the rest of the church family.

Do You Have Enough Commitment to Your Church to Stand with It Financially?

Many people in our churches will never understand the power of God in their financial lives. This is because many pastors backpedal when faced with this vital teaching responsibility. Paul told his disciples at Ephesus, "I didn't shrink from declaring all that God wants for you" (Acts 20:27). Our calling is to preach the whole counsel of God; this includes the philosophy of giving and tithing.

In our membership covenant, we lay a foundation for *future* teaching on tithes and offerings. We ask people if they believe in us enough to make our church their home. Then we ask them to make their new spiritual home the primary focus of their giving. During membership meetings we always mention the concept of storehouse giving. We underscore God's admonition to bring tithes and offerings "into the storehouse so there will be enough food in my Temple" (Mal. 3:10). We do not emphasize the word "tithe." Our goal is simply to invite partnership and help new members understand how their investment correlates to the ministry they enjoy.

Many people align themselves with a local church but direct their giving toward another nonprofit organization. The church is forced to supply their spiritual needs without the strength of their financial participation.

Are You Willing to Serve God Without Restraint?

This is the most demanding qualification for membership in Hope Chapel. Since 1984 we have defined our church as a team— Team Hope. Teamwork requires commitment to victory. No player on a sports field knows which moves he or she will need to make during a game. Likewise, no Christian can define limitations to their behavior while committing to serve God. We ask those who would join us to simply say yes to the Holy Spirit. We want them to tell the Lord that they will do whatever *He* asks of them. A yes to the Holy Spirit is not an automatic yes to the pastor or some other recruiter. Our goal is that everyone who calls him- or herself a member of our church would willingly go where the Spirit leads. This is not an attempt to manipulate anyone into service. It is perfectly fair for the member to turn down a specific request made by a pastor, staff member or other church member. We want obedience to God, not man or woman.

I always highlight the danger that lies inherent in this last question. No one ever became a missionary without first saying yes to some simple task in his or her home church. Membership in our congregation asks for faithfulness in the smallest things and an open heart toward larger horizons.

CHURCH PLANTER'S CHECKLIST

1. Write three paragraphs that define membership as you understand it.
2. List five to seven of the strongest metaphors for church membership in the New Testament. Strategize how you will salt your teachings and everyday speech with them.
3. Design a membership meeting. Your plan should include venue, schedule, interaction with staff, teaching content and new-member response.
4. Build a membership contract—keep it simple.

Note
1. Ralph Moore, *Friends: The Key to Reaching Generation X* (Ventura, CA: Regal Books, 2001), pp. 130-142.

PART 4

ANTICIPATING
the Future

CHAPTER 18

FOUNDATION:
HOW CAN YOU ENSURE
A HEALTHY START?

Football teams usually have a preset game plan. The coaches know the first 25 offensive plays they intend to run. The wisest coaches stick to their strategy. They do not allow circumstances, fans or players to deter them. Running those initial plays gives the coaches and players a feel for the opposition and for the general rhythm of the game. They save their adjustments for later in the contest.

Like a head football coach, as a church-planting pastor you need to stick to your game plan. This is not as easy as it sounds. A new church is a potpourri of ideas and methods. You and your core team will comprise a tactical unit in both thought and action. New converts will add their own spin to your plans. You will also face a cadre of people who transfer from other church-es. These people will bring their experiences with them. Many will offer great ideas that are worth consideration. Others will attempt to transport the traditions and methodologies that caused them to leave their former church home. Some will sim-ply bring along strategies that do not fit your new church.

Both good and bad ideas can be a distraction during the first few weeks of church life. Beware of anything that drives you off course. You have invested a great amount of time, energy, thought, prayer and hope into your plan. Protect it!

MODEL YOUR IDEAS

To work your plan, you will want to model your ideas with a few chosen leaders. This is where you can expand your core team to include zealous new recruits. Modeling leadership style is like building wooden forms for concrete. Whatever you do will last a long time. You then test your plan by operating it on a small scale. As your leaders watch and experience your leadership style, you become a role model for them to emulate.

How will small groups look? Will they be discussion groups or preaching points? Will they include singing or not? How will you make decisions—is consensus important or will a more top-down leadership style prevail? Who is your target audience? What systems and style will support your outreach to them? The list of questions goes on and should reflect everything we have looked at in this book. What is important is that those questions still have relatively the same answers three months into your church's existence as they did three weeks before kickoff.

Teach Systems and Long-Term Thinking
Avoid short-term solutions to long-term problems. Build and main-tain systems that reflect your values. Be sure to schedule and

conduct regular meetings for your staff and volunteers. These should be more than administrative meetings; they are teaching opportunities. Use them to inculcate new leaders with your values and plans. Operate them as systems-maintenance opportunities.

You might find yourself in a situation where a staff member got excited about a ministry they observed in another church. They propose doing something similar in your congregation. Use the opportunity to do more than just accept or reject the idea. Get your team to compare the idea to your statement of purpose, your vision and your needs. Use your time together to teach them how to think within the bounds of your philosophy of ministry. These discussions will strengthen your philosophy and further equip your team to face the future. In this way you glean far more than you would from treating the time as just another administrative session.

Project Stability
You will always want people to know that you have everything under control. Do not succumb to the temptation to swap strategies for whatever you found in the latest book you read or learned at the last seminar you attended. In fact, you should stay away from "ideation" opportunities until you are well in control of your game plan. Do not second-guess your own ideas without giving them time to bear fruit.

Think through and prepare stock answers for those who will want to change direction. Rehearse the answers until you can give them with a big smile, even if someone challenges you in anger. As I have already noted, publish your plans and refer to them whenever making decisions. These actions will bind your people together around a common vision and strategy.

Keep the Wineskin Flexible
While maintaining a steady focus on your vision, you also want to build flexibility into your new church. A game plan does not

prevent a defensive lineman from shifting his stance a few inches one way or the other. Nor does it prevent a quarterback from exploiting a weakness he finds in the defense of his opponents.

Innovation and change within the parameters of the game plan are your friends. They build freshness into the life of your congregation. Jesus compared religious groups with their traditions to wineskins. Made from the stomach of a sheep, these were supple at first use. Over time they would lose their flexibility. New wine in an old skin would cause the skin to "burst from the pressure, spilling the wine and ruining the skins" (Matt. 9:17). It is important to note that Jesus never criticized the old skin for being either *old* or well used. He simply addressed its inflexibility. Constant flexing is good for the wineskin of your new church.

Helpful Hint: Announce modifications to your leadership structure as "change for the better." This will help members see change as a positive step.

Create a Climate of Change

You can build an acceptance of change into the life of your congregation. The degree to which this prevails derives from your personal attitude toward change. If you view unexpected change (even for the worse) as an opportunity for God to show His faithfulness, then your people will be less bothered by it. At Hope Chapel, we once deliberately extended a small construction project over several weeks so that the congregation would come to church each week looking forward to a new change. We wanted to teach flexibility so that they could better handle the adjustments that we knew would constantly occur in a growing church.

Make it clear that you welcome change. This attitude pays off when you are forced to adapt to the needs of unchurched people around you. A congregation that resists change is more likely to spill the precious new wine of the Spirit than one taught to embrace change as a friend. There are always tidal waves of changes occurring in our culture. These impact the church and how we minister in our communities. The most *adaptable* congregations will continue as salt in the earth even during times of social upheaval.

Assume That God Will Meet Your Needs

One way to build flexibility into your thinking is to take God at His word. He said He "will supply all your needs from his glorious riches, which have been given to us in Christ Jesus" (Phil. 4:19). Assume that God will provide adequate resources, specifically meeting space, funds and leaders. This position of faith will cause you to innovate. If, on the other hand, you deny the adequacy of His provision, you will become a victim of complaining spirits.

At Hope Chapel, we hold six weekend services on Friday, Saturday and Sunday because we believe God gave us sufficient real estate to run our church. The alternative would be to complain that we need an auditorium large enough to hold the entire congregation at one time.

When we began services in Hawaii, several people joined us from a church that we had started several years earlier. The pastor was always complaining that he had no one capable of leadership. Among those ordinary members who came from that congregation, we found half of our first church council, a great counselor to alcoholics and a worship leader who set the tone for our church over the next two decades. Whatever the other pastor used as a screen to filter leaders had blinded him—he had overlooked these wonderful people. Because we believed that God supplied leadership in answer to our prayer for labor, we looked at those people in a different way than he did.

Financial resources for a church are always adequate. But many churches are often out of step with God's spending and harvesting plans. Sometimes a church's leaders will spend money unwisely, not thinking about its overall needs. Just as often, they ignore the Scriptures that pertain to income sources available to the church. You cannot pastor a financially successful church if you are not teaching Scriptures on tithes and offerings.

I have found that an apparent absence of resources always stimulates better vision. When this happens, I assume that I am missing something good that God has already made available. Prayer, Bible study, deep conversations and an understanding of the technical world help me when I reach this point. These factors collaborate to stimulate whatever new direction God is trying to communicate.

Sometimes planning and prayer lead to a different conclusion—that God is blocking a move. This seldom happens but is just as valid as the stimulation toward innovation and creativity. In either case the assumption of provision leads the way toward fresh understanding of God and His plans.

Build on Love

In *Love, Acceptance and Forgiveness,* Jerry Cook chronicles the early life of a successful fellowship he planted in Oregon (namely East Hill, where while caring for the yard, I had the epiphanic moment regarding church planting that I mentioned at the beginning of this book).[1] Jerry lived everything he taught. I remember complaining about a mentally impaired person who made noises during one of our meetings. Jerry told me that God sent the person to test us. If we were faithful with the least desirable people in our society, then we would be allowed to minister to those thought to be great. Over the years his lesson stuck in my heart. I have come to believe and teach that the way you can estimate the quality of a church is by observing how it treats its weakest member.

Our gospel is rooted in love. Our churches should reflect it. Teach your people to love, and they will generate innovative ministries to help needy people. They will also feel free to evangelize the unchurched. Fail to teach them to love broken people, and they will quickly become ingrown and judgmental.

Whenever Hope Chapel starts a new church, I encourage the pastor to look for a situation that will illustrate love and ingrain it into the life of the congregation. The spark may come through the simple testimony of a mentally handicapped person. It may come through the action of some very hip young man reaching out to help an elderly woman. It may be the pastor's own story of buying dinner for a homeless man.

In my current church, my friend and I went to dinner in the home of a family who had no stove. They ordered the food from a restaurant that evening. As we left that home, both of us were impressed that we should buy a stove for that family. Church funds were scarce; therefore, we purchased it out of our own pockets. Word eventually got around the church about our decision. Without any other teaching, our members began to share generously with one another. We believe God gave us the opportunity to buy the stove, knowing how our action would impact our church. *Ask Him for the drama that will set a loving tone for your church. He will provide it.*

Develop Momentum

As you go into your first public meeting, you will have momentum. It will be the product of all the plans you have laid. Momentum will exist in the hearts of your core-team members because everyone loves to see a plan come together. The grand opening of your church will add another layer of momentum.

You may suffer a temporary setback the second week, if your attendance drops. But fear not, this is normal. From the third week onward you should expect steady growth. You can enhance or detract from these gains by the decisions you make. Jesus said, "I will build my church, and all the powers of hell will not conquer it" (Matt. 16:18). Yet what the powers of hell cannot do, humans can easily accomplish by their own slow reactions. While He builds the church, the church planter needs to watch for and avoid logistical restraints that have the potential of restricting His work.

> **Helpful Hint:** Your job is to make sure nothing stands in God's way. You are much like the prophet's widow who found jars for Elisha to fill with oil (see 2 Kings 4:1-7). The only limit to the supply of oil was the number of jars.

Be Willing to Add Small Groups
New people will come to your church each week. Finding a place for them to fit will be one of your greatest challenges. There are, however, at least three remedies.

1. Build an apprenticeship into your leadership structure.
2. Invite apprentices into your training programs.
3. Appoint apprentices as home group leaders at an alarming rate. If your leadership team does not occasionally question your judgment, you are probably moving too slow.

Be Open When You Add Ministry Programs
Make individuals count more than programs. People's needs should not fall prey to your church structure. In a new church, there will always be cries to satisfy unmet needs and clashes between existing programs and certain individuals. Be sure to listen intently. Treat an idea or a complaint as the voice of God showing you where to move next. Also be sure to include the

person who raises the problem in any plans you make. Your job is to equip your people to do God's work. The best equipment may be a challenge to do something about the complaint. Many of our best ministry partners came to their assignment as complainers. My usual response goes like this: "The reason we are doing such a poor job in this area is because God never spoke to any of us about it, until he spoke to you. Now, what can I do to help you fill this need?"

Be Liberal When You Add Assignments

One way to make people feel welcome is to give them an assignment. Everyone wants to feel *needed*. At Hope Chapel, we try to subdivide jobs. A children's church teaching assignment can involve four adults rather than just one. We ask the primary teacher to recruit three helpers. One does crafts with the children. Another handles logistics involving attendance records and cookies. The third is a troubleshooter and can spend one-on-one time with superwiggly little boys. As I have already noted, ideally all recruiting is done from within the circle, and successors always come from within that team.

At Hope Chapel, we have actually found that multiplying assignments makes lighter work for everyone. It also creates better fellowship around the task. Most importantly, it gives more people an opportunity to know that their church family needs them.

Be Creative When You Add Space

You may find yourself scrambling for more classroom space for children or teenagers. You may need to provide counseling or prayer areas near whatever facility you use for weekend services. Your church may need adult training areas in addition to those you use for worship. Be creative. Think in terms of multiple facilities. You may rent two buildings on a Sunday. You may add tents for food service. Perhaps the alcoves of a public school will have to serve as classroom space. A real-estate office might provide a desk you can rent for a staff member. Office buildings often have conference rooms for rent. Many Kinko's stores have meeting rooms available for a fee. Be resourceful. But most of all constantly make room for growth as the Lord builds His church.

Be Ready to Add Services

As I have already noted, the easiest way to expand auditorium capacity is to add services. When you do this, never split a large congregation into two separate units. It is fun to worship in noisy crowded circumstances. Divide a "hot" crowd into two equal parts and you defeat momentum rather than enhance it. When adding an extra service, you should start independent of the established meeting. Begin as a pioneer group. Intentionally attract a small crowd, and do not provide for all of the peripheral needs at the first meeting. These might include greeters, nursery workers, food-service people, a full team of ushers and parking-lot attendants. Begin with the smallest crew possible. I have actually launched new services with no more than a single worship leader and myself. We recruited every other person from the crowd as it began to assemble. This gave each member a ground-floor experience. They went away feeling ownership and responsibility for the future success of the meeting. Let the new group recruit workers from among its members as needs arise. Recruiting as you go is easier than trying to build a big team all at once. Never ask the team from one service to duplicate its efforts at another. Recruitment from within will allow the new meeting to evolve its own personality rather than function as a knockoff of another.

Encourage the ministry team from one service to attend another, so their spiritual needs are met. Meeting spiritual needs in your ministry team is one of the best reasons for adding a second service. The needs of the volunteer team produce a good reason to have the senior pastor, or whoever speaks that day, preach at all services. The goal is to keep the whole church synchronized. This becomes even more important if you build your small-group ministry around the weekend message.

As You Grow, Add Parking

We have already looked at parking in this book. But it bears repeating. Aside from location, parking should be your greatest concern when choosing a facility. As you grow, stay informed about your parking problems. Count parking spaces, both the marked and creative ones. Count cars, so you know how many spaces are being used. Then count people, including children and infants. Divide the number of people attending by the number of cars that carry them. Multiply the quotient by the number of parking spaces. The final answer is your overall crowd capacity regardless of how many seats your auditorium will hold, unless you are in the inner city and close to public transportation that runs on Sundays.

If you rely on street parking, you should acquaint yourself with how far people are walking from their cars to your door. Compare this distance with other street-parking situations in your city or with the distance from the front door to the most distant spaces at your local discount store or Wal-Mart. You will not get people to walk much further than they are used to in other circumstances. Once you discern how far they will walk, inventory the parking within that radius. This is your virtual parking lot. Count the spaces and use the number for future planning.

As Ministry Expands, Add Staff

As you grow you will need to add staff, both paid and volunteer. When you look for someone to fill a role, remember that *form* is supposed to follow *function*. Do not hire people just because they are available, and do not qualify them only because of their credentials. Appoint them only if they have proven themselves *in the role* for which you need them. Hiring excellent volunteers is a way to be sure you are working with a motivated person. You will also know they can *do* the job. Remember that availability is not the same as ability.

If you are bivocational, you may want to hire staff before you pay yourself or at least before you go on full-time salary. Jack Hayford was dean of students at LIFE Bible College in Los Angeles when he started at The Church On The Way in Van Nuys. He hired students and a couple of faculty members as part-, then full-time, staff long before he resigned from LIFE to become full-time pastor. His actions ensured momentum to the rapidly growing congregation. I know a couple of bivocational pastors who oversee full-time staff and have no intention of giving up their secular careers.

Helpful Hint: Speed counts more than personal remuneration when you are trying to stay up with the momentum of church growth.

Let Your Leadership Build Morale

Morale is a product of leadership. You can build it. Start by letting your people know you are proud to be their pastor. Brag about their successes in your sermons. Find something your church can be the best at. Build goals around that phase of your work, and talk about it constantly. When you do this, you will lift every other area of ministry to the same level of excellence.

Make a long-term commitment to your congregation. Your people commit their trust to you. Remain worthy of it. Do not view your church as a stepping-stone to a larger assignment. God blesses lengthy pastorates—so will your people.

CHURCH PLANTER'S CHECKLIST

1. Write a plan for breaking your core team into three small Bible study groups. Then devise a plan to turn the three into nine groups. Add specific dates—now you have a schedule for growth.
2. Write an easy-to-say reply to the person who comes to you bubbling with an idea that will take focus away from your vision and strategy. Practice it until it you know it well.
3. Sketch out a six-panel brochure, including text and photos, that announces your vision, purpose and mission. Look for a professional who can turn your sketches into something beautiful.
4. On a scale of 1 to 10, rate yourself as a responder to change. Now write a strategy for teaching your church to respond positively to change.
5. List any growth-restricting obstacles that you can identify in the current version of your ministry plan. Devise three solutions for handling each hurdle.

Note
1. Jerry Cook with Stanley C. Baldwin, *Love, Acceptance and Forgiveness* (Ventura, CA: Regal Books, 1979).

CHAPTER 19

MINEFIELDS:
WILL YOU SURVIVE THE
FIRST FEW MONTHS?

When my wife and I started our first church, we learned some hard lessons about survival. Several experiences threatened the health of our church and our family. They ranged from mean-spirited people to physical illnesses. There was always the specter of fear threatening to overwhelm our faith. Since then, we have learned that a few precautions can prepare a church planter for the battle.

Most church planters are as inexperienced at taking new territory as we were. Lack of seasoning can translate into vulnerability to Satan's schemes. The goal of this chapter is to provide a little hard-won practical advice that will help you during the first few months in your new church.

GET READY FOR
THE SPIRITUAL WARFARE

You are on a mission that will change the face of history. There will be more people in heaven because you plant a church. Addicts will be set free. Suicides averted. Bankruptcies avoided. Men will become better husbands and fathers. Women will find their roles in the Lord and in their families. Children will enjoy childhood and reach adulthood with both parents in the house. If you are successful, you can glue a target to your forehead. You will not be popular on the opposing side of the spiritual battlefield.

Understand That the Battle Is Real

It is important for you to see the reality of spiritual warfare but in a proper balance. I am not necessarily suggesting that you cast demons out of buildings. Nor am I proposing that everyone who disagrees with you is Satan's messenger. But I do think that you should pay attention to the spiritual battles in the Bible. These range from Hezekiah's encounter with his enemies to Paul's thorn in the flesh to the carnality of the Corinthian church. Learn from these lessons because they are not relegated to biblical history. Be careful to arm yourself and stay alert in prayer, in discipline and in strategy.

Learn How to Discern Spiritual Warfare

Problems will always come and go. It is when they pile up that you should begin to wonder if you are not up against a spiritual foe.

We barely got started in our first church when my wife got pneumonia. The doctor said she was a danger to our infant son. I was on a speaking trip and got stranded in a snowstorm 500 miles away when she heard this diagnosis. We had little money. No relatives lived nearby. At first we simply thought we were surrounded by a combination of lousy circumstances. Our understanding grew quickly. Shortly after her illness we were blitzed by an obnoxious and antagonistic enemy. This attack came in the form of a person who did his best to undermine every decision made by our leaders. Life became even more complicated when I started getting weird telephone requests for counseling every Saturday evening. We prayed them off and then they began to occur on Thursday mornings as I prepared my messages.

The whole scenario was an assault against the church we were planting. We were able to identify it as coming from the enemy, because the problems all vanished quite quickly after we enlisted prayer support.

Pray, and Have a Positive Attitude
I have learned that there are two things you can do to withstand spiritual attack in addition to the advice you will find in Ephesians 6.

The first is to build a prayer team. Gather a group that you can access easily through e-mail. Keep them praying; it makes a difference. The second bit of advice is to maintain a positive attitude. Paul told the Philippian Christians, "Don't be intimidated by your enemies. This will be a sign to them that they are going to be destroyed, but that you are going to be saved, even by God himself" (Phil. 1:28). Their refusal to be intimidated was the weapon that would ensure their victory.

Let's take this a step further. Paul also announced that "God causes everything to work together for the good of those who love God and are called according to his purpose for them" (Rom. 8:28). If he was right, then we should truly rejoice in Satan's attacks because God will turn them for our good.

At Hope Chapel, some of our best ideas have come in response to Satan's attacks. One time we were locked out of public facilities in Southern California. Our dogged and prayerful efforts to use them resulted in those facilities being opened to other churches as well. I still rejoice that others have been blessed by our struggle. Satan's attacks can be worked "together for the good" if you handle them with alertness and faith.

EXAMINE AREAS OF ATTACK AND STRATEGIES FOR SURVIVAL

Forms of the struggle include sick children, inconsequential fights with your spouse and harassment just before you preach. Prayer is the ticket to victory over these kinds of problems and others.

There will be financial reversals. Be sure you become proficient at making and following budgets and build a financial backup system—I strongly suggest that you do not spend all of the money.

You will get the odd phone call from a nut who just will not let go. Unlist your home phone, and only answer your cell or office phone during advertised hours. Create a strategy whereby you do not offer counsel unless a problem comes through the recommendation of a small-group leader. If a person does not attend a small group, help them find one, but do not counsel them. If they refuse to hook up with a small group, then recommend them to a professional counselor.

Beware of "wannabe pastors." These are wolves in the flock who want to lead a flock but cannot make the cut. They might carry a theological degree. But their mission, intentionally or unintentionally, will be to make your life difficult. People like these—and they can be either male or female—are attracted to new churches because they think they can easily gain control. They usually have an unflattering history at a larger church where they are no longer welcome and find the smallness of a new congregation inviting. People such as these attempt to manipulate the pastor or leadership teams with generous financial gifts or promises. If people makes promises that seem too good to be true, ask their previous pastors about their track records. If you suspect wrong motives, hold off on giving them any ministry assignments. I even tell church planters to create a six-months-before-service rule. That rule states: We only assign ministry to people who have been involved with us for six months. You only haul out the rule when faced with a suspicious story. In every other case, you make the exception by putting the person to work as soon as possible, even on the first Sunday taking down chairs, as I noted earlier.

Another strategy is to put off the selection of a church board for one year. When you hastily appoint a board, you can lose your focus. Worse yet, you may select someone with secret ambitions that run contrary to your vision and leadership. However you choose a board, you should not seat one during the first 12 months of congregational life. Give yourself time to get to know the people who will control the direction and finances of the new church. Hopefully you come from a parent church. Ask their board to serve as a covering over you. They will not be inflicted with a need for control. Some new board member, whom you barely know, might have such an agenda.

Stick to Your Knitting

Stay focused on your basic goals. You have a game plan. Work it. Do not get distracted. Tom Peters in his wonderful book *In Search of Excellence* noted that one of eight shared characteristics of the 100 most-successful companies in America is their grip on a few core activities.[1] In other words, they stay focused. So should you.

Do Not Compete with the Government

The federal government feeds and houses the poor. They build schools. The government even gives away free money. You cannot afford to compete with them dollar for dollar, so give them their game and play another. Be involved, but do not get bogged down in social issues. Your primary job is to bring people into the kingdom of God and grow them to spiritual maturity. You are an equipper of Christians. Those you equip should involve themselves with the needs all around them, including social problems. They will function as lights in the world, especially if you teach them to do so *away from* the church campus. Not every ministry has to take place behind cloistered walls. We should send our people into the world to serve it. Also, not every ministry has to be funded by your church or bear your name. Stick to those things that are central to your calling.

Beware of the Feeder-Receptor Syndrome

Understand the feeder-receptor syndrome and its implications. I first understood this when I read a book by Carl George titled *Prepare Your Church for the Future*.[2] The idea is that large churches are very good at program development while small churches excel in evangelism. This is because most effective evangelism takes place through personal relationships. The big churches try to program evangelism thereby losing the relational aspect. While the large churches may be slower at evangelism, they are great at programs that nurture already-saved people. Hence there is a lot of transfer action between small and large congregations.

By definition, church plants are small but growing. You might spare yourself a lot of grief if you *do not* embark upon too many joint efforts with larger churches. This advice applies to everything, including evangelistic outreaches. I nearly destroyed momentum when we planted the first church. We immersed our leadership team in a great evangelistic crusade that touched much of Southern California. We surrendered our calendar and our energy to the larger organization, hoping to glean converts and learn skills from the project. Instead, we spent six months following the crusade rebuilding all that we had lost during that time. I believe those events are better left to the more established congregations.

There is another aspect to this that you should consider. We plant a lot of churches. Along the way, we have learned that we cannot invite our newer or smaller daughter churches to our outreach events, even though we multiplied our church to plant theirs. Every time we relent, too many of their members decide to join our congregations. We find ourselves hurting the very churches we most want to help.

> **Helpful Hint:** Small churches evangelize, big ones organize. Be sure you are not asking someone else to organize your converts.

Do Not Overcooperate

Peter Drucker, the management guru, teaches that corporate management owes a moral debt to customers and stockholders. That debt includes the ability to remain in business in the future. He says that when a person uses his or her position to exert leadership with social problems outside his or her purview, it is not statesmanship. Drucker deems it irresponsible behavior. He writes that overcooperation with just causes is irresponsibility if it in any way jeopardizes the existence of the organization a person is called to lead.[3] Just because there is a need in front of you does not mean that you have to fix it. There are needs all around you; if you try to fix them all, you will never fix any of them—you will only succeed in spreading yourself too thin and possibly missing God's voice. What you need to do is find out what God wants you to fix and go to work there.

As I have already noted, as a beginning pastor you will be invited to all kinds of partnerships. Some will seek to take money out of your congregation. Others will ask for large chunks of time from you or your members. Be selective. Do not join more than one pastors' prayer group and then only if it truly offers value. Do not become the denominational golden boy who accepts every volunteer job offered to him. Do not volunteer your members for tasks outside of your area of focus. Your priority lies with your own congregation and its needs. C. Peter Wagner calls overinvolvement in great activities "hypercooperation." He warns that it can kill any church.[4]

Early in our first church we gave away 15 percent of our income to poor people. This was in addition to denomination-al support, missionary giving and money we spent to plant churches. When we had the opportunity to buy a building, we felt we could not afford the payments. A wise pastor taught us to refocus our giving, and we bought the building. I am often invited to serve my denomination or community in ways that could easily be justified, but would jeopardize my time. I must constantly reassess and limit my involvement. I encourage you to do the same.

Protect Your Time

You must be in control of your personal schedule. I have already referred to this need in previous chapters, but let's look at some other elements you will need to include for your own good.

Set aside daily time with the Lord. Be sure no one—including your family—interrupts you. This is the bedrock that lies under all else that you will attempt.

After God, your time belongs to your family. Date your wife. Block out time with your children as you build your annual cal-endar. You have a limited amount of time to hang out with your kids. There are a finite number of family days or weekends avail-able before your children leave for college or get married. Do not waste a single one of them on ministry or any other noble pursuit.

Look after yourself physically and mentally. Get physical exercise, and pursue a hobby. Sharpen your mind by reading. I swim, ride a bike in the neighborhood and read simplistic detective novels whenever I take my nose out of a history book. The point is that you need to be a *person* if you are going to be a good pastor. Sacrifice yourself to the ministry, and there will be no more ministry. God wants healthy pastors, not living martyrs.

Make time to study and prepare the best messages you can present. You may not be the best preacher in the world, but you can certainly operate to the limits of your own capacity. Do not let your congregation steal the time you need to adequately prepare for Sunday morning. You should take time to form strategies and to read books pertaining to your ministry.

Everything you do in ministry will look like an emergency during the first few months. But most of it can wait. Your priorities must rule your calendar. We teach our young staff members that the only true emergency occurs when a person is in the hospital and dying. All other situations can wait while life's truly important foundational requirements are met.

CHURCH PLANTER'S CHECKLIST

1. How would you tell the difference between a mountain of problems and an attack from the enemy? What can you build into your new church to help withstand such attacks?
2. For which social needs should your church take responsibility? Which should you leave to the government?
3. List the 12 most anticipated uses of your time as pastor of a newly planted church. Prioritize them.
4. Create a "normal" seven-day calendar to serve as a guide for your personal life in the first six months of the new church. No two days should be exactly alike, but each week should closely resemble the others.

5. What percentage of time did you block out for personal interaction with God? With your family?

Notes

1. Tom Peters and Bob Waterman, *In Search of Excellence* (New York: Warner Books, 1982).
2. Carl F. George, *Prepare Your Church for the Future* (Grand Rapids, MI: Fleming H. Revell, 1992), pp. 31-34, 44.
3. Peter F. Drucker, *The Essential Drucker* (New York: Harper Collins Publishers, 2001), pp. 58-59.
4. C. Peter Wagner, *Leading Your Church to Growth* (Ventura, CA: Regal Books, 1984), p. 183.

CHAPTER 20

MULTIPLICATION:
CAN YOU BEGIN LIFE
AS A REPRODUCING
CHURCH?

I often ask Christian leaders, "What is the true fruit of an apple tree?" The responses vary. Some say apples, other point to the tree. Once someone said it was the apple core. The answer I look for usually comes late in the exercise. The true fruit of an apple tree is *an orchard.*

Every mature organism is capable of reproducing itself. Some do it many times. But most congregations will never do this in their lifetimes. The reason is that pastors think the fruit of their ministry stops with making converts. Most think of multiplying the number of Christians in their community. But we reproduce in kind. Christians should multiply converts. Churches should multiply congregations.

MULTIPLY YOUR MINISTRY

You will do the world a favor if you begin life as a reproducing church. By that I mean you should build vision for church multiplication into your congregation from the first week. Your core team should pray toward multiplication long before your first service. In the New Testament, James taught us that we "have not" simply because we "ask not" (4:2, *KJV*).

In our sixth month of existence, my congregation in Hawaii helped a parachurch group, whose leaders were attending our church, convert itself into a church plant. We planted our first daughter church on our first anniversary. Neither church would have been born if we had not been looking for opportunities to multiply our congregation. Our resources were extremely limited. Opportunistic vision compensated for lack of financial reserves. Simply believing in the possibility produced the fruit. Two decades later, both of these churches are still healthy.

Leverage Your Abilities

Multiplying the church will leverage your personal ability to minister to people. It is much easier to multiply leadership than to force the growth of a local church. Nearly 20 times as many people attend the churches in our "orchard" as attend the parent church. Such growth would have never happened if it had been confined to a single location.

Develop Low-Cost Missionaries

Church multiplication creates ends-of-the-earth opportunities for spreading the gospel without the costs associated with traditional missionary delivery systems. A local church can multiply itself much more cheaply across national boundaries than a denomination can place missionaries. Denominations must register with national and local governments. They are forced to warehouse enough money to bring all overseas personnel home in case of war or some other catastrophe. Bivocational church planters move in as private citizens, often sponsored by the companies that hire them. Because of their low overhead, they are free to focus on discipling a few people in a house or apartment. Planting churches through the network of a parent-church is like Johnny Appleseed criss-crossing America to form his ever-expanding orchard.

Outlast Yourself
Multiplying your ministry through church planting ensures that your life's work will continue after you retire or even after you die. Jesus expressed a desire not only that you bear much fruit, but that it be "fruit that will last" (John 15:16). Every congregation is vulnerable to shrinkage and loss caused by any number of factors. Misplaced leadership can kill a church. Rapidly changing demographics can mute a congregation if leaders are not open to quick change. I once saw a church stripped of 90 percent of its people through the defeat of the largest employer in that region. If your entire adult life had been invested in that church, you would have wished that you had spread your bets. There are antidotes to this vulnerability. Simply engage in making disciples and in multiplying churches.

Step Across Cultural Boundaries
God wants to cross cultural boundaries with His good news. Chances are that your community is a patchwork quilt of ethnic and cultural backgrounds. Most of the people in a multicultural neighborhood will not want to join your church. But if

you work with the few who feel comfortable crossing cultural lines, then you can raise up pastors to reach into the surrounding mosaic. The apostle Peter rode this principle into the house of Cornelius, spreading the gospel from Jews to Italians for the first time.

Grasp Your Greatest Opportunities

Pastors wear lots of hats. You are called to preach stunning sermons. You will quickly learn to excel in financial management. Crisis counseling will never go away, no matter how well you delegate. You will preside masterfully over romantic weddings and heart-rending funerals. Your roles as parent and spouse will soon call for lots of creativity. You are going to be a busy person. It is easy to lose sight of priorities in this very demanding position. But one role stands out above all the rest. It is making disciples—that task which presents the most opportunity for expansion of God's kingdom.

Make Discipleship a Priority

A pastor I know once told me how he had become frustrated. He is a very busy man. The church he serves pops with growth. There are more people to shepherd every week. He called to ask how to delegate the task of mentoring key leaders. I told him that I knew of no way to hand off his top priority. If you or I succeed at giving away our most important task, we will only accomplish the slow strangulation of our fruitfulness. I am not suggesting that you insert a new series of meetings into an overdriven schedule. It would be much better to incorporate discipleship into the administrative functions that draw you together on a regular basis.

Never forget that you are called to make disciples. Mentoring other people is top priority. Jesus' final instructions constrain you to make disciples. It is the only way of truly multiplying your ministry. But do not stop short. He also said to *go*. His plan was to reproduce the church in many locations.

Decide to mentor your disciples into solid Christians, and you will do so. Raise the bar a little. You will hit whatever targets you set for yourself. You can build the same people into strong leaders. So why not kick your standard a little higher? Try to focus on people who possess a capacity to multiply the Church. You mentor them while they mentor someone else. Ultimately your church will become a discipleship machine turning out lots of strong Christians. You can take the gospel to the entire planet in ways few others have dreamed.

CAREFULLY CHOOSE TEAM MEMBERS

I never choose people to work with me if I do not believe they can one day do my job. Making disciples is an investment. I would rather wait for a person with the ability to excel than fill a slot with someone capable of merely getting the job done. I am always looking for that individual with the capacity to launch another church.

It should go without noting that you would never select someone to disciple who is not a leader. It is easy to spot a leader. Look for followers. If you cannot easily identify followers surrounding an individual, you should not bet on that person—as a leader. Not everyone can function as a leader. It is those few who can who should eventually make it into the inner circles of leadership. They are the ones you will someday personally mentor. They are worthy of your priority commitment.

Catch the Vision
Potential church planters are vision catchers. They buy into the overall vision and mission of the congregation. Proof of this is a

willingness to sacrifice for group goals. Expertise does not qualify a person to work on a church staff. Fanaticism does. I still remember an event that took place in my high school speech class. One student gave a speech on weight lifting—he even brought the weights. The speech was supposed to last just five minutes. After he went on for 35 minutes, the teacher stopped him. Addressing the whole class, the teacher criticized the student for being long-winded while applauding him for his enthusiasm. The teacher dubbed the kid "a weight-lifting fanatic." He then taught us a proverb of his own making: "It is always easier to tame a monster than to create one." I always look for the "monster" when selecting people as my disciples.

Encourage Innovators

I want to work with innovative people. These are the change agents who will always find a better way to address culture as it changes around us. They are the visionary self-starters who keep our church and, at Hope Chapel, its aging pastor fresh. They keep us communicating to the next generation. I do not think of these as people who wear the latest styles. Ultrastylish people are often followers in disguise, as are the people who are always up on the latest trends in Christian circles. I am looking for original thinkers who can meld their circumstances with current events. They always invent new solutions and opportunities.

Look for Readers

I have already noted to you how important I think it is for you to be a reader. The more books you consume, the better. Good leaders must find ways to refresh themselves. When I was very small my father told me that I could learn about "anything in the world" in our local public library. Although I later discovered that my dad did not enjoy reading, I took him at his word.

Whatever we lack in ministry skills can be found in a book. Reading is especially important to the person we send into smaller rural areas or into cultures relatively unpenetrated by the gospel. Such individuals will have to find in books what they might otherwise learn from fellowship with other pastors. You can measure potential leaders in many ways. One of them is by asking about their reading habits.

Find Tough-Minded Thinkers

I look for tough-minded people. I only want to disciple someone who believes in their ideas enough to defend them. When I travel to Japan, I often hear what some call the national proverb: "The nail that stands up must be driven down." Japanese culture both honors and demands submission. I would rather find the nail that refuses to be driven down. This person may need shaping. They may need discipline. But from where I sit, that person looks a lot like the apostle Paul.

THINK MULTIPLICATION

We often overwork the concept of multiplication, but the Bible attributes roughly twice the fruitfulness to Elisha than it does to Elijah. Elisha's fruitfulness, of course, makes Elijah a winner. He did his job well at two levels. He prophesied faithfully, effectively and with supernatural results. He also mentored an effective disciple. If you add together the work of both men it totals three times the work of Elijah alone. Through Elisha, Elijah tripled his output. You can too, if you choose the right people and give them everything you have got.

I pray that your church succeeds. I hope that it becomes a megachurch in proportion to your community. But even more, I pray that your efforts will be multiplied in other places and beyond your lifetime.

Now glory be to God! By his mighty power at work within us, he is able to accomplish infinitely more than we would ever dare to ask or hope. May he be given glory in [your] church and in Christ Jesus forever and ever through endless ages. Amen (Eph. 3:20-21).

CHURCH PLANTER'S CHECKLIST

1. What three things could you do to program the *idea* of multiplication into your congregational DNA from the outset?
2. How can you raise the bar from enlisting converts to discipling future pastors?
3. Who among your core-team members look like future church planters?

Church Growth & Other Resources

Discovering MiniChurch: Small Groups That Really work
by Ralph Moore
Outline notes
6 audio tapes or 6 audio CDs

Discovering Advanced Church Planting
by Ralph Moore
Outline notes
8 audio tapes or 8 audio CDs

How to Hire, Fire & Manage In-Between
by Ralph Moore
Outline notes
6 audio tapes or 6 audio CDs

Let Go of the Ring: The Hope Chapel Story
by Ralph Moore
Paperback • 233 pages
ISBN: 0962812722

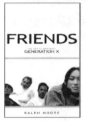

Friends: The Key to Reaching Generation X
by Ralph Moore
Paperback • 206 pages
ISBN: 0830728570

Facing the Realities of Science & Creation
by Ralph Moore
Outline notes
8 audio tapes or 8 audio CDs

How To Do MiniChurch: Growing From Within, Multiplying by Dividing
by Michael Kai
VHS Video

In God We Trust: Making Your Money Work For You
by Ralph Moore
Outline notes
4 audio tapes or 4 audio CDs

Available at Straight Street Resource Center
www.straightstreet.com • 808.235.5814

Church Growth Resources

Video Series

So You Want Your Church to Grow
by Ralph Moore
VHS Video

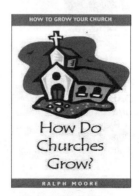

How Do Churches Grow?
by Ralph Moore
VHS Video

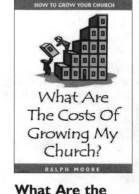

What Are the Costs of Growing My Church?
by Ralph Moore
VHS Video

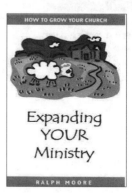

Expanding YOUR Ministry
by Ralph Moore
VHS Video

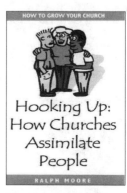

Hooking Up: How Churches Assimilate People
by Ralph Moore
VHS Video

Shepherding People in a Growing Church
by Ralph Moore
VHS Video

Available at Straight Street Resource Center
www.straightstreet.com • 808.235.5814